GEORGE MARSHALL

U.S.

WORLD LEADERS PAST & PRESENT

GEORGE MARSHALL

Wendy Lubetkin

CHELSEA HOUSE PUBLISHERS
NEW YORK
PHILADELPHIA

Chelsea House Publishers
EDITOR-IN-CHIEF: Nancy Toff
EXECUTIVE EDITOR: Remmel T. Nunn
MANAGING EDITOR: Karyn Gullen Browne
COPY CHIEF: Juliann Barbato
PICTURE EDITOR: Adrian G. Allen
ART DIRECTOR: Maria Epes
MANUFACTURING MANAGER: Gerald Levine

World Leaders—Past & Present
SENIOR EDITOR: John W. Selfridge

Staff for GEORGE MARSHALL
ASSISTANT EDITOR: Terrance Dolan
COPY EDITOR: Karen Hammonds
DEPUTY COPY CHIEF: Nicole Bowen
EDITORIAL ASSISTANT: Nate Eaton
PICTURE RESEARCHER: Alan Gottlieb
ASSISTANT ART DIRECTOR: Loraine Machlin
DESIGNER: David Murray
DESIGN ASSISTANT: James Baker
PRODUCTION MANAGER: Joseph Romano
PRODUCTION COORDINATOR: Marie Claire Cebrián
COVER ILLUSTRATION: Vilma Ortiz

First Printing

1 3 5 7 9 8 6 4 2

Library of Congress Cataloging-in-Publication Data

Lubetkin, Wendy.
George Marshall / Wendy Lubetkin.
p. cm.—(World leaders past & present)
Bibliography: p.
Includes index.
Summary: A biography of the military leader and statesman, discussing his roles in both World Wars and his service as a cabinet officer.
ISBN 1-55546-843-8
0-7910-0680-8 (pbk.)
1. Marshall, George C. (George Catlett), 1880–1959—Juvenile literature. 2. Generals—United States—Biography—Juvenile literature. 3. Statesmen—United States—Biography—Juvenile literature. 4. United States. Army—Biography—Juvenile literature. [1. Marshall, George C. (George Catlett), 1880–1959. 2. Generals. 3 Statesmen.] I. Title. II. Series.
E745.M37L83 1989
973.918'092—dc20 89–33127
[B] CIP
[92] AC

Contents

WORLD LEADERS PAST & PRESENT

John Adams
John Quincy Adams
Konrad Adenauer
Alexander the Great
Salvador Allende
Marc Antony
Corazon Aquino
Yasir Arafat
King Arthur
Hafez al-Assad
Kemal Atatürk
Attila
Clement Attlee
Augustus Caesar
Menachem Begin
David Ben-Gurion
Otto von Bismarck
Léon Blum
Simon Bolívar
Cesare Borgia
Willy Brandt
Leonid Brezhnev
Julius Caesar
John Calvin
Jimmy Carter
Fidel Castro
Catherine the Great
Charlemagne
Chiang Kai-Shek
Winston Churchill
Georges Clemenceau
Cleopatra
Constantine the Great
Hernán Cortés
Oliver Cromwell
Georges-Jacques Danton
Jefferson Davis
Moshe Dayan
Charles de Gaulle
Eamon De Valera
Eugene Debs
Deng Xiaoping
Benjamin Disraeli
Alexander Dubček
François & Jean-Claude Duvalier
Dwight Eisenhower
Eleanor of Aquitaine
Elizabeth I
Faisal
Ferdinand & Isabella
Francisco Franco
Benjamin Franklin
Frederick the Great
Indira Gandhi
Mohandas Gandhi
Giuseppe Garibaldi
Amin & Bashir Gemayel
Genghis Khan
William Gladstone
Mikhail Gorbachev
Ulysses S. Grant
Ernesto "Che" Guevara
Tenzin Gyatso
Alexander Hamilton
Dag Hammarskjöld
Henry VIII
Henry of Navarre
Paul von Hindenburg
Hirohito
Adolf Hitler
Ho Chi Minh
King Hussein
Ivan the Terrible
Andrew Jackson
James I
Wojciech Jaruzelski
Thomas Jefferson
Joan of Arc
Pope John XXIII
Pope John Paul II
Lyndon Johnson
Benito Juárez
John Kennedy
Robert Kennedy
Jomo Kenyatta
Ayatollah Khomeini
Nikita Khrushchev
Kim Il Sung
Martin Luther King, Jr.
Henry Kissinger
Kublai Khan
Lafayette
Robert E. Lee
Vladimir Lenin
Abraham Lincoln
David Lloyd George
Louis XIV
Martin Luther
Judas Maccabeus
James Madison
Nelson & Winnie Mandela
Mao Zedong
Ferdinand Marcos
George Marshall
Mary, Queen of Scots
Tomáš Masaryk
Golda Meir
Klemens von Metternich
James Monroe
Hosni Mubarak
Robert Mugabe
Benito Mussolini
Napoléon Bonaparte
Gamal Abdel Nasser
Jawaharlal Nehru
Nero
Nicholas II
Richard Nixon
Kwame Nkrumah
Daniel Ortega
Mohammed Reza Pahlavi
Thomas Paine
Charles Stewart Parnell
Pericles
Juan Perón
Peter the Great
Pol Pot
Muammar el-Qaddafi
Ronald Reagan
Cardinal Richelieu
Maximilien Robespierre
Eleanor Roosevelt
Franklin Roosevelt
Theodore Roosevelt
Anwar Sadat
Haile Selassie
Prince Sihanouk
Jan Smuts
Joseph Stalin
Sukarno
Sun Yat-sen
Tamerlane
Mother Teresa
Margaret Thatcher
Josip Broz Tito
Toussaint L'Ouverture
Leon Trotsky
Pierre Trudeau
Harry Truman
Queen Victoria
Lech Walesa
George Washington
Chaim Weizmann
Woodrow Wilson
Xerxes
Emiliano Zapata
Zhou Enlai

CHELSEA HOUSE PUBLISHERS

ON LEADERSHIP

Arthur M. Schlesinger, jr.

LEADERSHIP, it may be said, is really what makes the world go round. Love no doubt smooths the passage; but love is a private transaction between consenting adults. Leadership is a public transaction with history. The idea of leadership affirms the capacity of individuals to move, inspire, and mobilize masses of people so that they act together in pursuit of an end. Sometimes leadership serves good purposes, sometimes bad; but whether the end is benign or evil, great leaders are those men and women who leave their personal stamp on history.

Now, the very concept of leadership implies the proposition that individuals can make a difference. This proposition has never been universally accepted. From classical times to the present day, eminent thinkers have regarded individuals as no more than the agents and pawns of larger forces, whether the gods and goddesses of the ancient world or, in the modern era, race, class, nation, the dialectic, the will of the people, the spirit of the times, history itself. Against such forces, the individual dwindles into insignificance.

So contends the thesis of historical determinism. Tolstoy's great novel *War and Peace* offers a famous statement of the case. Why, Tolstoy asked, did millions of men in the Napoleonic Wars, denying their human feelings and their common sense, move back and forth across Europe slaughtering their fellows? "The war," Tolstoy answered, "was bound to happen simply because it was bound to happen." All prior history predetermined it. As for leaders, they, Tolstoy said, "are but the labels that serve to give a name to an end and, like labels, they have the least possible connection with the event." The greater the leader, "the more conspicuous the inevitability and the predestination of every act he commits." The leader, said Tolstoy, is "the slave of history."

Determinism takes many forms. Marxism is the determinism of class. Nazism the determinism of race. But the idea of men and women as the slaves of history runs athwart the deepest human instincts. Rigid determinism abolishes the idea of human freedom—

the assumption of free choice that underlies every move we make, every word we speak, every thought we think. It abolishes the idea of human responsibility, since it is manifestly unfair to reward or punish people for actions that are by definition beyond their control. No one can live consistently by any deterministic creed. The Marxist states prove this themselves by their extreme susceptibility to the cult of leadership.

More than that, history refutes the idea that individuals make no difference. In December 1931 a British politician crossing Park Avenue in New York City between 76th and 77th Streets around 10:30 P.M. looked in the wrong direction and was knocked down by an automobile—a moment, he later recalled, of a man aghast, a world aglare: "I do not understand why I was not broken like an eggshell or squashed like a gooseberry." Fourteen months later an American politician, sitting in an open car in Miami, Florida, was fired on by an assassin; the man beside him was hit. Those who believe that individuals make no difference to history might well ponder whether the next two decades would have been the same had Mario Constasino's car killed Winston Churchill in 1931 and Giuseppe Zangara's bullet killed Franklin Roosevelt in 1933. Suppose, in addition, that Adolf Hitler had been killed in the street fighting during the Munich *Putsch* of 1923 and that Lenin had died of typhus during World War I. What would the 20th century be like now?

For better or for worse, individuals do make a difference. "The notion that a people can run itself and its affairs anonymously," wrote the philosopher William James, "is now well known to be the silliest of absurdities. Mankind does nothing save through initiatives on the part of inventors, great or small, and imitation by the rest of us—these are the sole factors in human progress. Individuals of genius show the way, and set the patterns, which common people then adopt and follow."

Leadership, James suggests, means leadership in thought as well as in action. In the long run, leaders in thought may well make the greater difference to the world. But, as Woodrow Wilson once said, "Those only are leaders of men, in the general eye, who lead in action. . . . It is at their hands that new thought gets its translation into the crude language of deeds." Leaders in thought often invent in solitude and obscurity, leaving to later generations the tasks of imitation. Leaders in action—the leaders portrayed in this series—have to be effective in their own time.

And they cannot be effective by themselves. They must act in response to the rhythms of their age. Their genius must be adapted, in a phrase of William James's, "to the receptivities of the moment." Leaders are useless without followers. "There goes the mob," said the French politician hearing a clamor in the streets. "I am their leader. I must follow them." Great leaders turn the inchoate emotions of the mob to purposes of their own. They seize on the opportunities of their time, the hopes, fears, frustrations, crises, potentialities. They succeed when events have prepared the way for them, when the community is awaiting to be aroused, when they can provide the clarifying and organizing ideas. Leadership ignites the circuit between the individual and the mass and thereby alters history.

It may alter history for better or for worse. Leaders have been responsible for the most extravagant follies and most monstrous crimes that have beset suffering humanity. They have also been vital in such gains as humanity has made in individual freedom, religious and racial tolerance, social justice, and respect for human rights.

There is no sure way to tell in advance who is going to lead for good and who for evil. But a glance at the gallery of men and women in *World Leaders—Past and Present* suggests some useful tests.

One test is this: Do leaders lead by force or by persuasion? By command or by consent? Through most of history leadership was exercised by the divine right of authority. The duty of followers was to defer and to obey. "Theirs not to reason why / Theirs but to do and die." On occasion, as with the so-called enlightened despots of the 18th century in Europe, absolutist leadership was animated by humane purposes. More often, absolutism nourished the passion for domination, land, gold, and conquest and resulted in tyranny.

The great revolution of modern times has been the revolution of equality. The idea that all people should be equal in their legal condition has undermined the old structure of authority, hierarchy, and deference. The revolution of equality has had two contrary effects on the nature of leadership. For equality, as Alexis de Tocqueville pointed out in his great study *Democracy in America*, might mean equality in servitude as well as equality in freedom.

"I know of only two methods of establishing equality in the political world," Tocqueville wrote. "Rights must be given to every citizen, or none at all to anyone . . . save one, who is the master of all." There was no middle ground "between the sovereignty of all and the absolute power of one man." In his astonishing prediction of 20th-century totalitarian dictatorship, Tocqueville explained how the revolution of equality could lead to the "*Führerprinzip*" and more terrible absolutism than the world had ever known.

But when rights are given to every citizen and the sovereignty of all is established, the problem of leadership takes a new form, becomes more exacting than ever before. It is easy to issue commands and enforce them by the rope and the stake, the concentration camp and the *gulag*. It is much harder to use argument and achievement to overcome opposition and win consent. The Founding Fathers of the United States understood the difficulty. They believed that history had given them the opportunity to decide, as Alexander Hamilton wrote in the first Federalist Paper, whether men are indeed capable of basing government on "reflection and choice, or whether they are forever destined to depend . . . on accident and force."

Government by reflection and choice called for a new style of leadership and a new quality of followership. It required leaders to be responsive to popular concerns, and it required followers to be active and informed participants in the process. Democracy does not eliminate emotion from politics; sometimes it fosters demagoguery; but it is confident that, as the greatest of democratic leaders put it, you cannot fool all of the people all of the time. It measures leadership by results and retires those who overreach or falter or fail.

It is true that in the long run despots are measured by results too. But they can postpone the day of judgment, sometimes indefinitely, and in the meantime they can do infinite harm. It is also true that democracy is no guarantee of virtue and intelligence in government, for the voice of the people is not necessarily the voice of God. But democracy, by assuring the right of opposition, offers built-in resistance to the evils inherent in absolutism. As the theologian Reinhold Niebuhr summed it up, "Man's capacity for justice makes democracy possible, but man's inclination to injustice makes democracy necessary."

A second test for leadership is the end for which power is sought. When leaders have as their goal the supremacy of a master race or the promotion of totalitarian revolution or the acquisition and exploitation of colonies or the protection of greed and privilege or the preservation of personal power, it is likely that their leadership will do little to advance the cause of humanity. When their goal is the abolition of slavery, the liberation of women, the enlargement of opportunity for the poor and powerless, the extension of equal rights to racial minorities, the defense of the freedoms of expression and opposition, it is likely that their leadership will increase the sum of human liberty and welfare.

Leaders have done great harm to the world. They have also conferred great benefits. You will find both sorts in this series. Even "good" leaders must be regarded with a certain wariness. Leaders are not demigods; they put on their trousers one leg after another just like ordinary mortals. No leader is infallible, and every leader needs to be reminded of this at regular intervals. Irreverence irritates leaders but is their salvation. Unquestioning submission corrupts leaders and demeans followers. Making a cult of a leader is always a mistake. Fortunately hero worship generates its own antidote. "Every hero," said Emerson, "becomes a bore at last."

The signal benefit the great leaders confer is to embolden the rest of us to live according to our own best selves, to be active, insistent, and resolute in affirming our own sense of things. For great leaders attest to the reality of human freedom against the supposed inevitabilities of history. And they attest to the wisdom and power that may lie within the most unlikely of us, which is why Abraham Lincoln remains the supreme example of great leadership. A great leader, said Emerson, exhibits new possibilities to all humanity. "We feed on genius. . . . Great men exist that there may be greater men."

Great leaders, in short, justify themselves by emancipating and empowering their followers. So humanity struggles to master its destiny, remembering with Alexis de Tocqueville: "It is true that around every man a fatal circle is traced beyond which he cannot pass; but within the wide verge of that circle he is powerful and free; as it is with man, so with communities."

1

An Enlightened Act

June 5, 1947, was a pleasantly warm day for the 286th commencement exercises at Harvard University, in Cambridge, Massachusetts, and the young candidates for degrees could hardly have been more optimistic. World War II, in which many of them had fought, had ended two years before. They were back home, and the promise of rewarding careers in a healthy postwar economy lay ahead — the United States now held a startling 50 percent of the world's wealth. The depression had ended, the war was over, and the thoughts of young people were anywhere but in Europe. America's young men had fought on the road to Rome, on the beaches of Normandy, in the jungles of the South Pacific islands, and in the deserts of North Africa. Many had not come back. Those who had returned felt that they had done their duty and earned the right to turn their attention toward America and their own lives.

What we wanted most were fundamental ethics. We had witnessed what happens when the human mind is distorted by racism, terror, and violence. . . . America did not misuse its superiority by moral arrogance or political coercion, Marshall was not an ideologist, but a realist.

—RICHARD VON WEIZSACKER
West German president, at Harvard on the 40th anniversary of Marshall's speech

Secretary of State George Catlett Marshall (front row, third from the left) with fellow dignitaries in Harvard Yard after receiving an honorary degree from the university on June 5, 1947. That day, during his speech to the Harvard graduating class, Marshall made public his program for aiding the economic recovery of post–World War II Europe — the Marshall Plan.

Through the sea of caps and gowns and medal-bedecked military uniforms strode a man in an ordinary gray suit. In one of the commencement addresses the graduates would hear that afternoon, this man, Secretary of State George C. Marshall, would warn them that even now they could not turn their back on Europe.

Marshall had come to Harvard to receive an honorary degree. He was a modest man who hated publicity and displays of pomp. As chief of staff throughout World War II, he had brilliantly directed generals on all fronts, but he shied away from the limelight himself. He had accepted Harvard's offer only because he had a speech he wanted to make. It seemed the opportune time, and Harvard's 7,000 fresh-faced young graduates appeared to be the appropriate audience. In war, Marshall had been a man of great vision. England's prime minister Winston Churchill had called him the "organizer of victory." In his Harvard speech Marshall would show that he could turn his vision toward the preservation of peace, as well.

The American people do not, as a general rule, like or trust the military. But they like and trust George Marshall. This is more paradoxical than the fact that George Marshall hates war. The secret is that American democracy is the stuff Marshall is made of.

—*Time* "Man of the Year" article, January 1944

Few present at the ceremony realized how historic the moment really was. Some may even have dozed off in the afternoon sun as Marshall spoke the words that signaled a turning point in America's relationship with the rest of the world. It was a short and direct speech, characteristic of a man who had never been given to oratorical excess. Marshall began with an eloquently simple description of the plight of Europe.

The new technology used in World War II made it the most destructive war in history. By 1945, Europe lay in ruins. Air warfare had brought devastation to the cities of the Continent and to London and the British Isles. Industrial plants had been destroyed or stripped and converted for wartime use. Millions of acres of land had been laid waste, and the difficulties of reinvigorating the agricultural sector were amplified by poor weather conditions. The entire socioeconomic structure of Europe was disrupted. The victors had divided Europe among themselves, and much of what was once central Europe now fell into the Soviet sphere of influence. A

The West German city of Nuremberg, one of the many European cities devastated by Allied bombing raids during World War II. Following the conflict, Marshall, a career soldier, proved to be as adept at the art of peace as he had been at the art of war.

scar divided Europe down the middle; more and more it appeared it was a wound that would not easily heal. Europeans had no faith in their own currencies and even less in their governments. Communist parties were gaining a foothold in France, Italy, and Greece. By the spring of 1947 the situation had been made all the more critical by two of the worst winters in European memory.

All of this seemed very far away to the young men on that sunny day in New England. America was historically isolationist. The country had entered both world wars late and with great reluctance. When World War II ended, Americans wanted to return to their own affairs. They did not wish to become entangled yet again in the problems of nations that lay so far away, separated from North America by oceans and ideologies, but Marshall knew that giving the Allies victory was not enough. Europe still needed American assistance; this time not military but economic. Democracy in Europe could not survive in a situation of economic chaos, and Marshall had the foresight to recognize that America's future was inextricably tied to the future of democracy in Europe. "It is logical that the United States should do whatever it is able to assist in the return of normal economic health in the world, without which there can be no political stability or assured peace,"

George Catlett Marshall, Sr., was a successful and respected citizen of Uniontown, Pennsylvania. George, Jr., inherited his father's self-discipline and capacity for hard work.

Marshall told the graduates. He went on more boldly to promise, "Any government that is willing to assist in the task of recovery will find full cooperation, I am sure, on the part of the United States government." This was a sign that his intended audience was far broader than the 7,000 students assembled in Harvard Yard. Marshall was calling on the governments of Europe to participate in a "program designed to place Europe on its feet economically." And indeed, as Marshall spoke, his undersecretary of state, Dean Acheson, was busy making certain that the Europeans received and understood this invitation. That night, before going to bed, the British foreign secretary, Ernest Bevin, read what he immediately realized was an "exceptionally important speech."

The nations of Europe were prompt with their response to what came to be known as the Marshall Plan. (It appeared, at the start, that even the Soviet Union would be interested; but the division between East and West had already become too wide, and it was not to be.) Scarcely over a year later, $4,875 million in Marshall aid was made available to the countries of Western Europe. America had taken on the responsibility for peace and economic stability in the postwar world.

Marshall had been invited to Harvard to speak as a great general, the man who had assembled the world's most powerful army and sent it to win history's most destructive war. The citation read to him at Harvard referred to Marshall as "an American to whom freedom owes an enduring debt of gratitude, a soldier and statesman whose ability and character brook only one comparison in the history of this nation." That other American, who went unnamed, was George Washington. Nobody seemed to feel that this praise was excessive; they rose to give Marshall a standing ovation. But henceforth the great general's name would be tied to a great act of peace rather than war. The Marshall Plan would make the economic recovery of Europe possible, and without that recovery America's prosperity would not last. Journalist Walter Lippmann called it an "act of enlightened self-interest."

George's mother, Laura Marshall, set an example of patience and stoic good humor for her family, qualities that would enable her younger son to survive the mental and physical rigors of a soldier's life.

George C. Marshall was born on December 31, 1880, to Laura Emily and George Catlett Marshall, in Uniontown, Pennsylvania. The town of his birth was a kind of minor crossroads of American history. Since Uniontown was first laid out in 1776, Lafayette, Andrew Jackson, and Henry Clay were said to have visited or passed through. Just about 10 miles from the Marshalls' home was Fort Necessity, where George Washington fought the first battle of the French and Indian Wars. But, as George Catlett Marshall, Sr., liked to remind his children, the Marshalls had an illustrious history of their own. Proudly displayed in the family library was a book, *The Marshall Family*, which traced their roots back into the deep soil of colonial Virginia and Kentucky. George C. Marshall, Jr., could claim to be an indirect descendant of the great chief justice of the Supreme Court, John Marshall. But the boy preferred another legend (probably untrue), which claimed that one 18th-century Marshall maiden had married the infamous pirate Blackbeard. Later, George C. Marshall would disparage his family's fascination with its own roots: "I thought the continual harping on the name of John Marshall was kind of poor business. It was about time for somebody else to swim for the family."

George Marshall, future chief of staff of the U.S. Army, at five years old. Marshall enjoyed a wholesome and relatively carefree boyhood in his hometown of Uniontown, Pennsylvania.

At first it appeared that it would be his older brother, Stuart, who would make the Marshall family proud. Laura Emily and George Catlett Marshall, Sr., had four children, the first of whom, a boy, died at the age of six months. There was a daughter, Marie, who was four years older than George, and of course Stuart, the eldest, who was six years older than he. Stuart was the apple of his father's eye. Although George, Sr., was affectionate with George, Jr., his youngest son always felt that his poor academic record was a disappointment and embarrassment to his father, who was an ambitious and successful businessman as well as a prominent member of the local Democratic party. George, Jr.'s relationship with his mother, however, helped to soften some of the tension between him and his father. Laura Emily Marshall was a good-natured and understanding woman, and she was careful never to pass judgment on young George. She always reacted to her son's boyhood peccadillos and tribulations with humor rather than anger, and this provided the basis for the stoic philosophy toward life that George would display in his adult years.

And although George, Jr., was indeed a mediocre student, there was one subject that was an exception; Uniontown was so rich in history that it could hardly fail to fire the young boy's imagination. "If it was history," Marshall later recalled, "that was alright: I could star in history."

Young George also excelled at boyish hooliganism. One episode he recounted with pleasure to his official biographer, Forrest Pogue, involved a makeshift ferryboat. George and some other boys began charging the girls from the neighborhood to be ferried across a narrow stream. One day the girls boarded the boat but refused to pay. "I was terribly humiliated," Marshall recalled, "and what made it worse, my chum Andy began laughing at me and my engineer and boon companion began laughing at me and I was stuck. Just then my eye fastened on a cork in the floor of the boat which was utilized in draining it. With the inspiration of the moment, I pulled the cork and under the pressure of the weight of the passengers, a stream of water shot up in the air. All the girls screamed and I sank the boat in the middle of the stream. They all had to wade ashore. I never forgot that because I had to do some-

From left to right are the three Marshall children: Marie, Stuart, and George. George and Stuart never got along; although Stuart was their father's favorite, he was insecure and envious of his younger brother.

George Marshall, Sr., sent a letter to an old friend at the Virginia Military Institute (VMI), Brigadier General Scott Shipp, to alert the general to the arrival of young George and to ask him to keep an eye on the new cadet.

thing and I had to think quickly. What I did set me up again as the temporary master of the situation."

Temporary master was correct, for there was heck to pay at home when George's father heard about the incident. On this occasion, as on many others, George, Jr., was ushered down to the basement for a beating with the willow stick his father kept there (and whose sting Stuart often seemed to be spared).

The vivid military history of the region in which he grew up probably influenced George in his decision to become a soldier. Given his poor academic record, West Point was out of the question. Marshall was accepted, however, at another respected military school, the Virginia Military Institute (VMI), at Lexington, Virginia, where his brother, Stuart, had studied. Although George's mother and father were opposed to the idea of a military career for him, they agreed to VMI because it offered courses such as engineering and Stuart's major, chemistry. One person who remained opposed to the idea of George attending VMI, however, was his older brother. One day George overheard Stuart talking to his mother.

"He was trying to persuade her not to let me go because he thought I would disgrace the family name. . . . The urgency to succeed came from hearing that conversation; it had a psychological effect on my career."

The life of a cadet at the school George so wanted to attend was anything but easy. VMI might offer a variety of courses of study, but in its routine it was true to its name. As one of the first-year cadets, known to the older boys as "rats," George had to undergo hazings, sleeping in dormitories with the windows open in midwinter, and an indescribable staple dish in the school mess known as "growlie." It was in his first year at VMI, ragged by the other boys as the "Yankee rat," physically weak from a bout with typhoid, that Marshall began to exhibit the stoicism that would distinguish him later in his career. He never complained and said later, "I think I was more philosophical about this sort of thing than a great many boys. It was part of the business, and the only thing to do was accept it as best you could."

Cadets holding commissioned rank at VMI pose for a group photograph in 1900. Seated in the front row (third from left) is Marshall, who had already risen to the rank of first captain and commander of Company A.

Two things particularly affected Marshall during the four years he spent at VMI. The first was the beginning of the Spanish-American War in 1898. Since 1895, Cuban insurgents had been fighting a war of independence against the Spanish authorities. (Cuba was a Spanish colony at the time.) In the United States, the sympathy of the public was with the Cuban nationalists. In February 1898, the USS *Maine* was sunk in Cuba's Havana Harbor. The United States blamed Spain and took advantage of the incident by demanding independence for Cuba and declaring war on Spain. U.S. soldiers fought Spanish troops in the Philippines, where the U.S. Navy destroyed the Spanish fleet in Manila Bay, and in Cuba. The result of the conflict was the cession of most of Spain's remaining overseas colonies to the United States. Young cadet Marshall, with a burgeoning awareness of international affairs, realized that the war signaled the beginning of America's expanding international role, and he hoped to be involved in that role in some way.

After war, what affected the young Marshall most during those years was love. Just past the gates of the academy lived Elizabeth ("Lily") Carter Coles.

Lily Carter Coles, the belle of Lexington, Virginia, was admired by most of the cadets at VMI, but it was the courtly young Captain Marshall who attracted her attention.

Descended from one of Virginia's founding families, Lily had the charm, the beauty, and the lineage to make her the belle of Lexington. She was well known to the cadets of VMI and had had flirtations with more than one of them, including George's brother, Stuart. But among the many men who showered her with attention, Lily had not found one she wanted to marry. Not until she met George Marshall, that is.

By now Marshall was a tall and handsome young man with a proud bearing and striking blue eyes. His confidence had been enhanced by his academic success in his major field at VMI, civil engineering, and he had been promoted to the rank of first captain. He had gained the respect of his fellow cadets and his superiors. Lily may have first heard about him when her mother entertained members of the VMI faculty. One evening, out for a stroll with some companions, George heard a piano being played beautifully in Lily's house. Lily, he later reminisced, "was the finest amateur pianist I have ever heard." He returned to the house on several occasions to stand outside and listen to her play. One evening Lily invited him in.

By the time Marshall graduated in 1901, he and Lily had reached an understanding. Engaged to such a beautiful and talented woman, George was more determined than ever to live up to her and his own expectations. Despite his study of civil engineering and his parents' persistent opposition, Marshall was still set on a military career. His father acquiesced, and seeing that his son's "whole heart was in it," set about trying to use his considerable political influence to secure a commission in the U.S. Army for George. Young George tried pulling a few strings himself. In an act that would be unimaginable today, he marched into the office of the president of the United States, William McKinley, to state his case. Marshall was certain that he was allowed to stand for examination because of that short interview, although he was later unable to recall exactly what McKinley had said. The president was no doubt impressed by the young man's self-confidence.

What I learned at VMI was self control, discipline, so that it was ground in. I learned also the problems of managing men.
—GEORGE MARSHALL

THE PRESIDENT OF THE UNITED STATES OF AMERICA

To all who shall see these presents greeting:

Know Ye, That reposing special trust and confidence in the patriotism, valor, fidelity, and abilities of George C. Marshall, Jr. I have nominated, and by and with the advice and consent of the Senate do appoint him Second Lieutenant of Infantry in the service of the **United States:** to rank as such from the second day of February, nineteen hundred and one. He is therefore carefully and diligently to discharge the duty of Second Lieutenant by doing and performing all manner of things thereunto belonging.

And I do strictly charge and require all Officers and Soldiers under his command to be obedient to his orders as Second Lieutenant. And he is to observe and follow such orders and directions, from time to time, as he shall receive from me, or the future President of the United States of America, or the General or other superior Officers set over him, according to the rules and discipline of War.

This Commission to continue in force during the pleasure of the President of the United States for the time being. **Given** under my hand at the City of Washington, this eighteenth day of January in the year of our Lord one thousand nine hundred and two and in the one hundred and twenty sixth year of the Independence of the United States.

By the President: Theodore Roosevelt

Elihu Root
Secretary of War.

2

New Frontiers

Before he could be commissioned into the U.S. Army, Marshall had to pass a series of examinations in New York. He did, though he had to wait almost three months for the results. Shortly after December 31, 1901 (his 21st birthday), Marshall was made a second lieutenant. A few days later, he learned that he would be stationed in the Philippines, which had become U.S. territory after the Spanish-American War. If he and Lily were to be married before he left, they would have to move with great haste. Within a span of a few short weeks in February 1902, Marshall took two great oaths: The first was taken before a notary public in Uniontown, when he received his commission on February 3. The second was taken just eight days later, before a pastor of the Episcopal church, at the Coles's home in Lexington, when he married Lily.

He always struck me as a curiously Roman figure, something of the type of a Roman general who flourished in the days of the Republic.
—CLEMENT ATTLEE
British prime minister

Following his graduation from VMI in 1901, George Marshall, with the help of his father and President William McKinley, secured a commission to the U.S. Army. George Marshall, Sr., initially objected to a military career for his son, but when he realized that George's heart was set on it, he used his political influence to obtain a commission for George.

The 21-year-old Marshall was commissioned to the U.S. Army as a second lieutenant in the infantry, and thus was launched one of the most distinguished careers in the history of the U.S. armed forces.

The wedding was an informal affair arranged with great haste because of Marshall's impending departure. Just the two families and a few friends were there. Even Stuart attended, although he and his younger brother had finally fallen out for good. Stuart had been in the room when George first told his family about Lily. Apparently what the older boy had to say about his former girlfriend was far from flattering. Marshall would never repeat what was said on that occasion, but he refused to attribute his estrangement from his older brother to rivalry over Lily. "You know perfectly well we were never congenial," he told his goddaughter, Rose Page, when she ventured to ask him about it years later, "and that Stuart opposed everything that I wanted to do, including my marriage to Lily."

Lily and George had only a few short days to spend on their honeymoon before the new second lieutenant was to set sail from San Francisco on the *Kilpatrick*. They spent that time in Washington, D.C., but the thought must have always been with them that once George left he would not be home again for at least two years. It was also during their abbreviated honeymoon that Marshall learned that his wife was suffering from a weakness of the heart. She was a semi-invalid who would never be able to have the children her husband longed for. But Marshall was stoic as always in his acceptance of this, and he continued to be deeply in love with Lily.

The Philippine Islands, a former Spanish colony, had been occupied by the United States during the Spanish-American War. Spain's cession of the islands to the United States was followed by the brief rebellion of a group of Filipinos seeking independence under the rebel leader Aguinaldo. But before Marshall left the United States, the rebellion had been crushed, and William Howard Taft had been appointed the first American civilian governor of the Philippines. Just a day after he arrived in the city of Manila, Marshall was dispatched to the island of Mindoro. It was hardly a paradise that he discovered when he disembarked from the army launch *Isla de Negros*. The island's capital, Calapan, was a cluster of native huts on stilts, surrounded by dense tropical jungle. The troops he was to command,

Marshall later recalled, were "about the wildest crowd I've ever seen before or since." Although the islands were more or less peaceful when Marshall arrived, the threat of death hung over them in another form. A cholera epidemic had begun on the islands about two months before Marshall arrived. The disease was fatal in almost all cases. In Calapan, Marshall faced the difficult task of keeping his unruly troops confined to their barracks and making certain that even under the primitive conditions on the island they followed the rigid procedures of hygiene that prevented the spread of the disease.

In July, Marshall was transferred to Mangarin, at the southern end of Mindoro, where he discovered that he would be in charge of the company stationed there and would act as civil governor for the area until a superior officer arrived in September. It was a great deal of responsibility for a young officer, but although some of his subordinates found him inexperienced, Marshall managed.

Before Marshall departed for his post in the Philippines, he and Lily were married. The members of the Marshall-Coles wedding party are (left to right) Marie Marshall, the bride and groom, Stuart Marshall, George's mother and father, and Lily's mother.

Company G of the U.S. Army's forces in the Philippines. The Philippine islands had been ceded to the United States following the Spanish-American War; the U.S. military presence was needed to suppress rebel Filipinos who wanted independence for their native land.

Six months had passed since he had left Lily and the United States behind for the primitive and isolated life of a remote Philippine island. Mail was delivered to the island only once a month, along with meager rations. "There was no turkey, chicken, or fresh vegetables. Fried peaches and apples and desiccated potatoes were a daily ration. No ice in a tropical hot sun," Marshall recalled later, describing the grueling start of his career in the military.

In December, shortly before his 22nd birthday, Marshall was transferred with his detachment to far more amenable surroundings near Manila. He moved into a comfortable army house, which he shared with about 10 other officers, spent pleasant evenings with them in Manila's Army and Navy Club, and learned to ride horseback, the form of recreation he would favor throughout his life. The months in Manila provided a much-needed respite before the last of Marshall's assignments in the Philippines — which was in many ways the worst. In September 1903, his company was sent to Malahi Island to join a detachment guarding military prisoners there. The island was a suitably depressing site for a prison housing the "dregs of the Army of the Philippine Insurrection," as Marshall called them. Malahi had a no less somber effect on the spirit of the soldiers who were assigned to watch over them. The prisoners, who Marshall thought were the toughest men he had ever seen, spent their days quarrying rock and their nights sleeping naked on rows of metal cots. Marshall remembered the relief of his company when they were allowed to leave just a little over a month after being posted there. They were replaced by another infantry unit freshly arrived from the United States. "Their depression when they saw the place was very great," said Marshall. "Our elation when we left was even greater."

Marshall's elation must have vastly increased when he learned that the Thirtieth Infantry, to which he belonged, had been ordered home. His next assignment would be on the American frontier, at Fort Reno, an army post west of Oklahoma City in Cheyenne Indian country. But first, Marshall was granted a painfully brief disembarkation leave, during which he visited Lily in Lexington, where she was still living with her mother. To his great disappointment he found his wife in too frail a condition to accompany him to Fort Reno. But the

The tropical environment in the Philippines was an inhospitable one. Dysentery, cholera, and malaria were rampant, decent food and drink were scarce, and the troops under Marshall's command were surly and frequently fought among themselves.

tedium of life at Reno, which must have made him miss Lily even more, was broken scarcely more than a year later by a more interesting assignment. In June 1905, Marshall set out on a mapping expedition to the heart of the Texas badlands.

As always, Marshall was stimulated by a fresh challenge, and this job, he later said, was "the hardest service I ever had in the army." Through the hottest months of midsummer, Marshall and his team traveled an unforgiving landscape in which water and forage for their horses and mules were hard to come by. In July, the worst month, temperatures soared above 130 degrees, and rations of onions and potatoes were exhausted. Nothing was left but unappetizing canned meats. Marshall believed that he lost at least 30 pounds during the trip. When the mapping expedition arrived in Langtry, Texas, Marshall's sergeant felt that he had earned a break. After receiving his paycheck, he barricaded himself in the town's bar and brothel and refused to let any other Langtry residents in. It was only through Marshall's intercession — an early act of ad hoc diplomacy — that the sergeant was finally swayed to share the establishment with the townspeople.

Marshall spent the summer of 1905 commanding an army surveying expedition in the Texas badlands. The members of the expedition braved 130-degree temperatures to complete a detailed map of the area.

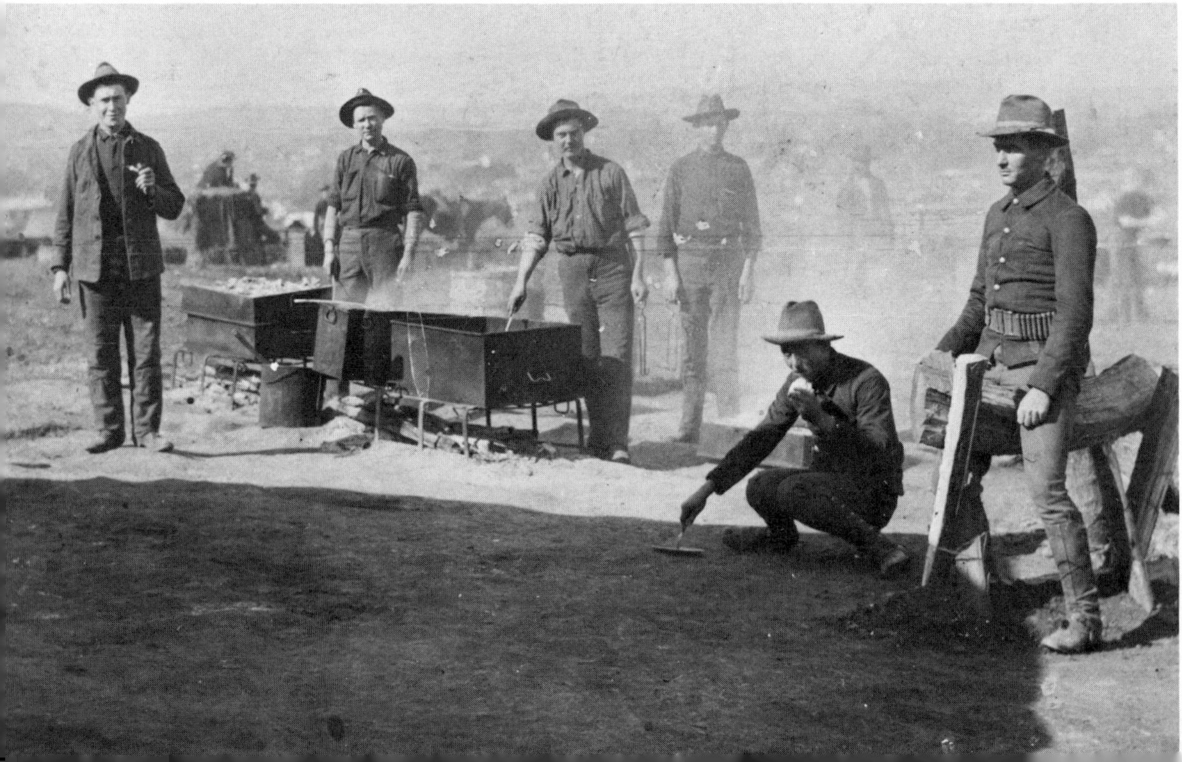

Finally, three months later, the scruffy, sunburned group of men and animals straggled back to the base camp at Fort Clark, Texas. Marshall later remembered that the captain at headquarters could hardly believe Marshall was an officer when he saw him "burned almost black" and "wearing an old Panama hat which a mule had bitten the top out of." But the young lieutenant's efforts were twice rewarded. His map was praised as "the best one received and the only complete one," and he was given four months' leave. After three and a half years of separation he and Lily would finally be able to spend a considerable amount of time together.

Early in 1906, Marshall returned to Fort Reno with Lily, who was feeling well enough to accompany him. But their stay there would be a short one; Marshall was offered admittance to a four-year program at the Infantry and Cavalry School at Fort Leavenworth, Kansas. The school had been opened in 1902 to provide training for officers who were seen fit to assume higher command. Marshall found his position at Leavenworth "a little ticklish" because he was the only second lieutenant at a school intended for captains and majors. "I was a bit discouraged at the start," he later admitted. "I hadn't any preparation. . . . And so I knew I would have to study harder than I had ever dreamed of studying in my life. And I just worked night and day. My great trouble was going to sleep at night." If Marshall's nerves were a bit on edge, it was because he rightly recognized that this was the career break he had hoped for. His hard work and sleepless nights paid off in the end: He finished first in his class.

The years at Leavenworth were formative ones for Marshall. Among his classmates and instructors at Leavenworth were many men with whom he would be associated in later life. At Leavenworth he made a casual acquaintance with another student, future five-star general Douglas MacArthur, and with Lieutenant Colonel Hunter Liggett, under whom he would serve in the Philippines and during World War I in France. On a personal level, he suffered a loss that would make him feel that with one blow his youth had ended. In 1909, George C. Marshall, Sr., died suddenly of a stroke.

Brigadier General John ("Black Jack") Pershing, in a photo taken during his punitive expedition against Mexican bandit-rebel Pancho Villa in 1916. Marshall considered Pershing, who would lead the American troops in World War I, the ideal soldier.

Lieutenants Bruce Palmer (left) and George Marshall take a break during engineering class at Fort Leavenworth, Kansas, in the spring of 1907. Marshall attended the Infantry and Cavalry School there from 1906 to 1911.

After graduating from Leavenworth in 1911, Marshall wanted to take Lily on the extended honeymoon they had never had. And somehow, although the Marshalls were living on a shoestring budget, the young lieutenant managed to scrimp and save enough for a holiday in Europe. After the vacation, the pace of travel hardly abated. Over the next two and a half years, Marshall would be posted in Arkansas, Massachusetts, New York, Minnesota, and Texas. And then came a call for another move across the Pacific. Marshall was assigned to the Thirteenth Infantry, stationed near Manila. He would be based at Fort McKinley, which had been built from the stones he had watched men quarry at the prison camp on Malahi.

George and Lily Marshall arrived in Manila on August 5, 1913, to find the situation in the Philippines somewhat tense. Japan had annexed Korea in 1910, and now the United States watched Japan with suspicion, wary of what that act of aggression might forebode for the Philippines. The troops at Fort McKinley were engaged in maneuvers designed to test the U.S. ability to defend the island. In one of these, a simulation of the invasion of the island of Luzon (on which Manila is located), Marshall would demonstrate the depth of his tactical and organizational talents. After one of the leaders of the mock invasion fell ill, Marshall took over, although he was only a junior lieutenant. So impressed was one of the men who took part in the maneuvers, Lieutenant Henry ("Hap") Arnold (who would become chief of the air forces during World War II), that he accurately predicted in a letter to his wife that this was a man with the makings of a future chief of staff. Many other men noticed Marshall's fine performance in the Philippines that fall and winter. His biographer, Forrest Pogue, noted that it "gave a dazzle to Marshall's name."

During his years at Fort Leavenworth, Marshall became acquainted with many of the men who would eventually form the brain trust of the U.S. military, including World War II hero Douglas MacArthur.

Despite the crisis that was building up in Europe and that soon led to the outbreak of World War I, the concern of the American army and public during this period was focused on the Mexican border. In March 1916, the rebel Mexican Pancho Villa led a raid across the border into the United States and killed American soldiers and citizens in Columbus, New Mexico. Brigadier General John J. Pershing, the man whom Marshall would come to admire above all others, pursued Villa back across the border into Mexico. Although he chased him for 11 months, Pershing failed to catch the wily Mexican revolutionary.

The British passenger liner *Lusitania* departs from New York in May 1915. The trip would be the *Lusitania*'s last; German submarines torpedoed and sank the ship — with all passengers — shortly thereafter.

U.S. borders had been violated, and the perpetrator had gone unpunished. A feeling of frustration with America's military impotence was beginning to build up. It was exacerbated in May 1915 when the British passenger liner *Lusitania* was sunk by German submarines operating in neutral waters of the Atlantic. (The Germans claimed the ship was carrying arms and other war supplies and were later proved correct.) American lives were lost, and many voices were now raised demanding that the United States toughen up its military forces. Previously, the nation's armed forces had been structured along individual state lines. President Woodrow Wilson began advocating a genuinely national force that could stand up to such affronts to the nation's sovereignty. In June 1916, partial reform was begun when Congress passed the National Defense Act. Among its provisions was the establishment of summer camps at which professional men could spend a few months preparing for the possibility of military service.

It wasn't as if brains didn't exist in the Army at that time, but it was just hazardous to use them. You followed the book.

—GEORGE MARSHALL
on the intransigent quality of the army during the peacetime years prior to WWI

It was to one of the most scenic of these camps that Marshall returned from the Philippines in 1916. The Citizen Military Training Program was voluntary, and the men who entered it had to pay for the training they received. The program had a reputation for laxity, and Marshall, who had just been made a captain, was instructed to put some muscle into one of the most notoriously pleasant of all the camps, located in the resort town of Monterey, California, at the Del Monte Hotel. It was fashionable for young men of society to spend a few months in the program. "They were all the hot bloods of San Francisco," remembered Marshall. "I saw more Rolls Royces and other fine cars around there than I had ever seen." The new captain quickly gained a reputation for toughness among the men; they nicknamed him Dynamite Marshall. In the meantime, increasing German aggression in the Atlantic and heightening tensions in Europe lent urgency to Marshall's attempts to whip his men into some kind of shape. He sensed that war was not far off.

3

The War To End All Wars

When Archduke Franz Ferdinand, the heir to the throne of Austria-Hungary, was assassinated by a Serbian nationalist in Sarajevo, Bosnia, on June 28, 1914, there were few in the United States who believed that this remote and isolated incident would give rise to the First World War. (Bosnia was part of the Austro-Hungarian Empire at the time; it is now one of the six constituent republics of Yugoslavia.) But tensions in Europe had been growing for a long time. In the late 19th century the balance of power on the Continent had tilted precariously eastward. After a period of extraordinary growth between 1860 and 1871 and the unification of the nation under its chancellor, Otto von Bismarck, Germany emerged as a major industrial and military power. As the old balance vanished, a new structure of alliances came into existence, with France, Britain, Russia, and eventually the United States and Italy — called the Allied powers once the war broke out — pledged to support one another against Germany and Austria-Hungary (called the Central Powers during the war). With this structure in place, the spark at Sarajevo quickly became a conflagration.

If we had fought by the book rules, we would have wrecked ourselves about every 20 minutes.

—GEORGE MARSHALL
on the World War I
campaign in France

Marshall (standing, on the right, with other members of General Pershing's staff) arrived in France in June 1917 as a captain in the First U.S. Army Division — the first American division to set foot on European soil during World War I. By the end of the war in 1919, Marshall was a full colonel and the personal aide to General Pershing.

Archduke Franz Ferdinand (center, facing camera), the heir to the Austro-Hungarian throne, was assassinated by Serbian nationalist Gavrilo Princip on June 28, 1914, in Sarajevo, Bosnia. The assassination initiated the chain of events that led to the outbreak of World War I.

The United States entered the war on April 6, 1917. Its new allies were in a desperate situation, and President Wilson was very anxious to send troops to Europe as soon as possible. In the meantime, a military delegation under Major General John J. Pershing was dispatched to France. Marshall longed to be assigned to the delegation, but it was not to be. The young captain did manage to be part of the next best thing, however. In June 1917, he set sail on the *Tenadores* with the First U.S. Army Division, which was the first American fighting division to set foot on French soil during the war.

World War I was supposed to be the war to end all wars; the one that would make the West, in President Wilson's words, "safe for democracy." But people were unprepared for the destructiveness of modern warfare. The eager young American troops could not have imagined the horrors that awaited them on the front stretching from the English Channel to the Swiss frontier: the foggy battlefields strewn with mines and barbed wire; the muddy, corpse-filled trenches; the clouds of poisonous gas.

Despite the National Defense Act and the Citizen Military Training Program, U.S. troops were anything but prepared. Some of the men who sailed to France on the *Tenadores* had just been issued their rifles and did not know how to use them. They would have to be trained in France.

The French were delighted by the arrival of the American troops but impatient that they get down to the real business of helping win the war. French morale was extremely low. Shortly before the arrival of Pershing and his staff, the French had suffered a devastating defeat and 95,000 casualties after launching an offensive against the Germans along the Aisne River. It was hoped that the presence of American troops fighting side by side with the French would boost the spirits of the beleaguered French forces.

President Woodrow Wilson and his second wife, Edith Galt Wilson, at the World Series in 1915. At the outbreak of World War I, Wilson advocated a policy of neutrality for the United States; by 1917, however, Wilson had declared that America must enter the war in order to make the world "safe for democracy."

The Allies wanted to integrate the Americans with the British and French units, who already had experience in training troops and who argued that they could get the Americans into combat more rapidly that way. But Pershing was determined that the U.S. Army remain a self-sufficient unit even if it meant a greater delay before U.S. troops were actually seen in the trenches. A presidential directive had given the prestigious major general freedom to organize the American Expeditionary Force (AEF) in France as he saw fit. But it explicitly stated that "the forces of the United States are a separate and distinct component of the combined forces, the identity of which must be preserved."

French soldiers aid a fallen comrade in the trenches of the western front during World War I. The use of poison gas made trench warfare a particularly hellish experience for troops on the front lines.

One of Marshall's first encounters with Pershing reflected the icy personality of the major general. Black Jack Pershing was the quintessential military man. He was tough, combat hardened, uncompromising, and occasionally ruthless. Marshall already had great admiration for the man who had chased Pancho Villa's guerrilla band across Mexico. But Marshall was not the type of soldier who would be tongue-tied by his admiration for a superior if he felt there was something that had to be said.

Pershing made frequent short-notice visits to the First Division from his own offices at Chaumont. He was suspicious of the competence of Marshall's commanding officer, General Sibert, and some believed that Pershing intended to find an excuse to relieve him. Marshall's loyalty to Sibert was stirred during a Pershing visit on October 8. Pershing grilled Sibert — in front of his staff — about an exercise that Marshall had organized. When Sibert was unable to answer completely, Pershing turned away from him contemptuously. At this point, Marshall spoke up. "General Pershing," he began, "there's something that has to be said here and I think I should say it because I've been here the longest." Pershing stopped for a moment to listen to the younger officer defend Sibert. When Marshall had had his say, Pershing stated evenly, "You must appreciate the troubles we have," and turned to walk away. But Marshall, "having gotten into it up to my neck," called after him. "Yes, General, but we have [troubles] every day and they have to be solved before night."

Marshall's friends were certain that with those words he had put an end to his career. But, in fact, they were the beginning of a mutual respect that would grow between the two men. Marshall later commented, "It was one of [Pershing's] great strengths that he could listen to things." Pershing was the man Marshall admired most throughout his career and one of the few he allowed to address him informally as George. Not long after his confrontation with Pershing, Marshall was promoted to major.

Major General William Sibert, commander of the U.S. Army First Division in France during World War I. Marshall served under Sibert as a captain and then as a major during his first months in Europe.

Artillerymen of the First Division of the American Expeditionary Force in France pose in front of the cannon that fired the opening shot of the U.S. effort in World War I, on October 23, 1917.

In November 1917, the first Americans to die in France were buried with great honor in French soil at the village of Bathelemont. On October 21, American troops had been sent, still inadequately prepared, into the trenches. To give them a taste of the war, but not too bitter a taste too soon, they were assigned to an area north and west of Nancy, which had been relatively quiet. Unexpectedly, in the wee hours of November 3, the Germans advanced. After detonating a Bangalore torpedo (a special explosive device used to break through the trenches), 40 or 50 Germans surprised the Second Battalion of the Sixteenth Infantry. Three Americans, Corporal Gresham, Private Enright, and Private Hay, were killed in the ensuing struggle, and 12 others were taken prisoner by the retreating German troops. General Bordeaux, the commander of the French Eighteenth Division, alongside which the Americans had fought that night, delivered a moving tribute at the funeral for the three men. He concluded by asking that "the mortal remains of these young men be left here, be left to us forever. We will inscribe on their tombs: Here lie the first soldiers of the famous United States Republic to fall on the soil of France, for justice and liberty."

By early 1918, the Allied position had worsened considerably. In 1917 two successive revolutions had occurred in Russia, which threatened the Russian commitment to the eastern front. On March 3, 1918, the leader of the Communist October Revolution, Vladimir Lenin, faced with problems enough establishing his new government in Russia, signed peace terms dictated to him by the Germans. Once Russia withdrew, the Germans would be able to mass 250 divisions in France, where they would face an Allied force of only 150 divisions. The Germans realized that the United States was speeding up its delivery of troops to Europe — 85,000 new recruits arrived in March and 120,000 more in April — so they were desperate to launch an offensive before the AEF could get itself organized.

The German assault came as soon as weather permitted, in March, before the Americans were ready to take positions alongside the Allies on the western front. The blow the Germans dealt the Allies was almost fatal. As Marshall wrote in his memoirs, "Few Americans will ever realize the situation of the Allies

Military funeral services held in November 1917 at Bathelemont, France, for the first three Americans to be killed in action on European soil during World War I. By war's end, these 3 would be joined by 116,516 other American soldiers.

Seated from left to right at the Paris Peace Conference of 1919 are Vittorio Orlando of Italy and the chief architects of the Treaty of Versailles, the "Big Three" — David Lloyd George of Great Britain, Georges Clemenceau of France, and Woodrow Wilson of the United States.

at this particular period of the war. The Fifth British Army, virtually demolished, had been replaced by French reserves and these in turn were suffering severely. The enemy had made a penetration of sixty kilometers and had cut the principal railroad artery between the British and French. . . . During the onrush of the Germans there was one period of twenty-four hours when serious consideration was given to the plan of carrying the French line due west to the coast, and abandoning all effort to keep in touch with the English. The most severe loss, however, was in the morale of the English infantry, which for a time was very low."

General Pershing realized that the situation was so dire that he would have to relent on his insistence on a separate American army. The war might be lost while the Americans trained. At Chaumont-en-Vixen, Pershing told the troops, "We come from a nation that for one hundred and fifty years has stood before the world as the champion of the sacred principles of human liberty. We now return to Europe, the home of our ancestors, to help defend those same principles upon European soil." Marshall believed that in that moment Pershing "rose to greatness." The general now agreed to send Americans into combat as part of a combined Allied counteroffensive. They would be scattered along 400 miles of front under French command. "Temporarily jeopardizing his own and even American prestige, he laid all his cards on the table and directed every move toward the salvage of the Allied wreck," Marshall wrote in his memoirs. "In the midst of a profound depression he radiated determination and the will to win."

In mid-May the U.S. Army made its first offensive, at Cantigny. It was a tiny village but an important possession for the Germans because it was situated on a plateau and made a good lookout. Pershing realized that if the U.S. troops were successful here it would raise the faith of the French and British in the fighting capabilities of the Americans. Such a victory would have an important impact not only on the French and British but on the Germans as well.

Marshall helped plan the offensive at Cantigny, which was launched in the early morning of May 28. "The general artillery bombardment opened with a tremendous roar and Cantigny itself took on the appearance of an active volcano, with great clouds of smoke and dust and flying dirt and debris," wrote Marshall. In a matter of a few hours, a single regiment of the First Division was able to take the town. "The success of this phase of the operation was so complete and the list of casualties so small that everyone was enthusiastic and delighted, but this reaction was of short duration, for troubles were coming thick and fast." Over the course of the next month the Germans maintained a series of fierce counterattacks, determined to recapture the town. In Cantigny, the First Division lost almost 200 soldiers that May.

As a staff officer, Marshall did not live in the mud but he was up at the front frequently and acquired a deep and abiding sympathy for the infantry that he never lost.

—FORREST C. POGUE
American historian

Pershing believed that the sacrifices at Cantigny were worth making and proved that the U.S. troops and staff were the "equal of any." But while the First Division was holding on to Cantigny, a third and more threatening German offensive heated up and pressed toward the Marne River. After just eight days of fighting, the Germans stood on the right bank of the river. On the other side lay Paris itself. The Germans began an attempt to cross. French marshal Ferdinand Foch, head of the now unified Allied army, was impressed by the mettle American troops had shown at Cantigny. He called on the Second and Thirty-fourth U.S. Divisions to help stop the enemy at the Marne. At Belleau Wood and Château-Thierry, two of the decisive battles of World War I, the American forces helped turn the tide against the Germans.

Marshall's excellent work with the First Division led to his promotion to the rank of temporary full colonel. He hoped that he would soon be in command of a battalion of his own. But on July 12, 1918, four days after he left Cantigny, George Marshall received orders to report for service at Pershing's general headquarters in Chaumont. On the same day, the First Division received orders to move to the southeast, but no one knew what was in store for them there. Because they had just come from the hard fighting at Cantigny, it was believed that they would probably be kept in reserve positions away from the actual combat. Marshall had to bid a hurried farewell to the men with whom he had been associated for over a year in France. In his memoirs he remembered seeing them "gathered in the broad doorway of the chateau. The friendly jests and affectionate farewells . . . made a deep impression on my mind, and I drove off hardly daring to wonder when and where would be our next meeting."

> ***The thing that stands out in everybody's recollection of General Marshall is the immensity of his integrity, the loftiness and beauty of his character.***
>
> —DEAN ACHESON
> American statesman

As Marshall took up his new responsibilities in the operations section at Chaumont, the war was reaching a turning point. On July 18, 1918, the Germans' last great offensive was reversed. The Second Battle of the Marne, a counteroffensive at Soissons spearheaded by American troops, brought on the retreat of the German army from that area. Six days after he left them, Marshall's First Division took part in that historic and bloody Allied offensive and "within seventy-two hours every field officer of the infantry, excepting three colonels, had fallen." Had Marshall been granted his wish to lead a battalion into combat, there is a good chance that he would not have survived.

At Chaumont, Marshall found himself "in a strange atmosphere." From the harsh life-and-death realities of the western front he had come to a place of military abstraction. Questions of ocean tonnage, ports of debarkation, and construction of docks and great depots filled the minds and the conversations of the men at headquarters. Marshall was not happy about being moved to general headquarters. However, it was here that he would have a chance to make a name for himself as a brilliant administrator and tactician. The new job also provided excellent experience for the man who would later oversee such matters on a global scale as chief of staff during World War II.

In the midst of the final Allied drive toward the German positions at Saint-Mihiel, Marshall had to turn his attention to planning the move to the new front. Over 600,000 men, 2,700 field guns, and 900 trucks would travel north by night. They could be routed over only three open roads to a destination that all had to reach within two weeks. Pershing was skeptical that it could be done. Faced with the impossible, he turned to Marshall. After the war, Marshall wrote with pride about the successful execution of the move, which earned him the nickname "wizard": "Despite the haste with which all the movements had to be carried out, the inexperience of most of the commanders in movements of such density, the conditions of the animals and the limitations of the roads, the entire movement was carried out without a single element failing to reach its place on the date scheduled, which was, I understand, one day earlier than Marshal Foch considered possible." As the troops moved toward Meuse-Argonne, Marshall received notification that he would soon be promoted to the rank of colonel.

[Marshall] never tricked anyone. He never made a promise to a man, woman, or child that he did not keep. In a world of overpaid heroes and untrustworthy politicians, is it possible that one man made it to the peak and still kept his principles?

—LEONARD MOSELY
Marshall biographer

By the fall of 1918, the Central Powers were broken and the war was over. Although Woodrow Wilson had called for a "peace without victors," the French were pushing for an occupation and for heavy reparations to be paid by the Germans. Wilson relented and agreed to many of the vindictive terms set down by French president Clemenceau. The Treaty of Versailles, one of the most justifiably maligned documents in diplomatic history, laid the groundwork for the events that would lead the world to war again 20 years later.

Marshall (far left) and three fellow officers with their landlady, Madame Jouatte (seated at left), and members of her family at Gondrecourt, France, where Marshall was billeted in 1917. The gracious Madame Jouatte provided Marshall with all the comforts of home during his stay with her.

With the end of the war came the dawning of the jazz age. Marshall had a quick prelude of that brief but giddy epoch in the round of victory celebrations that followed the armistice. It must have been grand to be young, handsome, and an American officer in Europe after World War I. The French and British were falling all over one another in their eagerness to express their gratitude. In late April 1919, Marshall and other members of Pershing's staff were to receive the French Legion of Honor award at a ceremony in Metz. Just before the presentation of the awards for distinguished service, Marshall was approached by a member of Pershing's staff, who was bearing an invitation that would affect the next five years of the colonel's life. "How would you like to be the General's aide?" Marshall was asked.

Soon Marshall was off with Pershing for victory celebrations in Paris and London. After a triumphal parade in Paris, the general and his staff departed for England, where they would be feted by heads of state and royalty. Marshall was dazzled by the charming women of British high society. "I walked around quite a while with Lady Curzon who is supposed to be one of the beauties of London," he wrote in the diaries he kept of that extraordinary week in England. "She introduced me to a number of people, and pointed out all those who occupied important positions." Every evening there were dances, and Marshall loved to dance. Despite his serious nature, the young officer was caught up in the carefree exuberance of the times. At one party his head was turned by the duchess of Sutherland, with whom he shared the last three dances of the evening. "She is really beautiful, dances extremely well, and is quite delightful to talk to," he wrote in his memoirs. "She is at the head of the Queen's household, and occupies the first position in England after royalty." Royalty and grace on the dance floor did not always go hand in hand, Marshall learned after a whirl with Princess Mary. "If she doesn't reign any better than she dances, they are in a hard way," he wrote of the princess.

Back in France, Pershing and his homesick men packed up quickly. As they boarded the *Leviathan* to sail for home, preparations were under way in Washington, D.C., and New York to welcome the returning heroes in style. Soon Marshall would be reunited with Lily, whom he had not seen for over two years, and with whom, despite the beautiful ladies of the British court, he was still very much in love.

At the pier in Brest, Marshal Foch had parting words for the Americans, words that hinted at the future: "We have cemented our ties of friendship," he said in his farewell speech, "and if ever in the future we shall find it necessary to unfurl our banner, then we know that we shall continue as brothers-in-arms." But that was a future America did not want to contemplate in 1920. The slogan of the moment and of the successful Republican presidential candidate Warren Harding was A Return to Normalcy. The decade that followed would prove to be America's last great period of innocence and irresponsibility.

4

Heart and Hope

Study the first six months of the next war.
—GEORGE MARSHALL
from his dictum
at Benning

No sooner was the war over than Congress began demanding defense cutbacks. The controversial March-Baker bill, which Congress was deliberating, had been drafted by Pershing's archrival Peyton March, who held the only job that the iron-willed general coveted — chief of staff. As endorsed by the secretary of war, Newton Baker, the bill called for an army of half a million men. Pershing was to deliver a recommendation on it to the Joint Senate and House Military Affairs Committee on October 31, 1919. Marshall helped Pershing prepare for his testimony, in which he would argue that a regular army of 275,000 to 300,000 was adequate. The report that the two men prepared helped in the passage of the National Defense Act of 1920, which authorized a peacetime army of just under 300,000 men.

Pershing soon got the job to which he had been aspiring. Not long after Warren Harding took office, Pershing was appointed chief of staff; he took office on July 1, 1921. The general and his staff were installed in the State, War, and Navy Building in Washington, D.C. Pershing, who traveled abroad

Following the end of World War I, Marshall (right) was given a chance to work closely with his mentor, General John J. Pershing (left). Black Jack Pershing was already a near-legendary figure in America and Europe; he would become the only six-star general in U.S. history.

frequently, relied heavily on his chief aide, George Marshall. The chief of staff respected Marshall because he always stood his ground. Marshall, even when he disagreed with his boss, continued to respect him above all others. Later, he wrote to Pershing, "My five years with you will always remain the unique experience of my career."

The move to Washington finally gave Marshall and his wife a chance to settle down for a few years. Since returning from Europe, Marshall had been on the move so much that Lily had remained with her mother in Lexington. Now the couple was assigned quarters at Fort Meyers, near the capital. Marshall, who loved children but would never have any of his own, became godfather to a little girl who lived nearby, Rose Page. Rose spent a lot of time with the Marshalls and in her memoirs described how devoted George was to his wife: "He showered Lily with a hundred little attentions. He fetched and carried. He planned little surprises. He was ever solicitous about her health and comfort." As normalcy had come to the nation, so it had at last to the couple's domestic life. Lily Marshall, however, despite her outward cheer and healthy appearance, was still a very sick woman.

I am not a diplomat. I mean exactly what I say and there is no use trying to read between the lines because there is nothing to read there.
—GEORGE MARSHALL

As the end of Pershing's term as chief of staff approached in 1924, Marshall applied for an assignment with the Fifteenth Infantry, which was stationed in Tientsin, China, to protect U.S. commercial and industrial interests there. He was growing older and needed to spend time commanding troops in the field if he was ever to advance to the rank of general (which his former classmate from Leavenworth, Douglas MacArthur, already held). Marshall's only regret when his request was granted was that he would have to say good-bye to Rose. Lily and her mother would accompany him to Tientsin.

Marshall disembarked in China on September 7, 1924. He had arrived during one of the most complex periods in the country's turbulent history. The last emperor of the Manchu dynasty had abdicated in 1912. A republic was founded, but the structure of power in China, with independent warlords controlling vast areas of the countryside, foiled at-

Lily Marshall at the Tientsin railroad station in China, in September 1926. Despite her poor health, Lily accompanied her husband on his three-year tour of duty in China. She died in 1927, shortly after their return to the United States.

tempts at unification and democratization at every turn. In 1924, Dr. Sun Yat-Sen was president of the republic, but his power base was limited to the south. It was difficult to know who controlled the north, where three formidable warlords, Chang Tso-lin, Wu P'ei-fu, and Feng Yu-hsiang, kept the balance of power shifting. Meanwhile, a struggle between Sun's brother-in-law Chiang Kai-shek and Communist leaders was beginning, a conflict that would plague China for decades to come. (When Marshall returned to China in 1945, he would find that in spite of 20 years of seemingly interminable bloodshed on Chinese soil, the same contenders for power were as intransigent as ever.)

Because the new commanding officer of the Fifteenth Infantry had not yet arrived in Tientsin, Marshall was the temporary chief. Almost as soon as he debarked from the *Thomas*, which had carried him to China after a stopover in Manila, Marshall was faced with his first crisis. Since August the warlords Chang Tso-lin and Wu P'ei-fu had been fighting in northern China. Wu and his army of 100,000 began retreating in the direction of Tientsin. They had to be disarmed and prevented from plundering the city —a task that fell to the American forces.

Marshall's solution to this problem was typically ingenious. He organized five outposts around Tientsin where American soldiers would offer Wu's hungry troops a meal in return for their weapons. "Make it plain to them," Marshall instructed the men at the posts. "You give arms, we give food. No guns — no rice." Although Marshall's troops were vastly outnumbered by Wu's army, the maneuver was successful. In a letter to an old friend, Marshall confided, "I snaffled a nice letter of commendation out of the affair which is worth my three years in China."

Unfortunately, the Fifteenth's commanding officer, Colonel Naylor, arrived a few months later. He was jealous of Marshall's success and determined to make his subordinate's position clear to him. From taming warlords' troops Marshall now had to turn to tempering the morals of the men. The Fifteenth Infantry had one of the highest rates of venereal disease in the army. One payday, Marshall wrote to Pershing (with whom he corresponded regularly), "We are up against the problem of cheap liquor and cheaper women." Marshall attacked the problem with the same common sense and tactical skill he displayed throughout his career: He had rickshas stationed outside the bars the men frequented, making it easy for them, once the bars closed, to return to the barracks instead of spending the night in a local brothel.

Despite the tedious duties Naylor assigned him, Marshall enjoyed life in China. He applied himself to learning the language and soon felt that he was better at it than he had been at French. He also made a study of the Chinese military and noted that although the discipline among Wu P'ei-fu's troops was only fair, their equipment was quite modern.

To keep fit he took long morning rides on a shaggy Mongolian pony he had trained and played tennis in the afternoons at the American Tennis Club. Lily Marshall and her mother discovered a shoppers' paradise in the bazaars of Tientsin. One manual for infantrymen who were to be posted to China warned that in the course of a China tour the serviceman's wife "invariably accumulates a rather impressive store of rugs, silver, linen, lingerie, embroideries and other impedimenta that would be utterly beyond his means if priced on Fifth Avenue."

Marshall was not enthusiastic about his next assignment, which was to teach at the Army War College in Washington, D.C. Just two months before the Marshalls were to leave Tientsin, Naylor, an alcoholic, was removed from command. Marshall once again had the exhilaration of running the show and was sorry to leave. But Lily was "radiant over the idea of a beautiful house at the Washington Barracks." Soon after moving in, however, Lily became ill. Her heart condition had been complicated by a disease of the thyroid and she would have to undergo a serious operation. Initially, it appeared that the operation was a success. On September 15, 1927, while George was lecturing at the War College, Lily's doctor told her that she would be allowed to go home the next day. A week earlier she had written relatives that her one desire was "to get *home*." On the morning of the 15th, filled with excitement, she rose from bed and went to her desk to start a letter to her mother — a letter that she would never finish. Just after nine that morning Marshall was called from his lecture to a telephone. The guard who had summoned him remembered that Marshall "spoke for a moment over the phone, then put his head on his arms on the desk in deep grief."

The death of his wife shattered George Marshall's world. A month after her death he turned to the only person he thought would understand. General Pershing had lost his wife and three daughters in a fire that swept through his home in 1915 while he was in El Paso. Now Marshall wrote to him, "The truth is, the thought of all you had endured gave me heart and hope. But twenty-six years of most

. . . the most brilliant, interesting, and thoroughly competent collection of men I have ever been associated with.
—GEORGE MARSHALL on the men who taught at Benning during his last three years there

intimate companionship, something I have known ever since I was a mere boy, leaves me lost in my best efforts to adjust myself to future prospects in life. If I had been given to club life or other intimacies with men outside of athletic diversions, or if there was a campaign on or other pressing duty demanding a concentrated effort, then I think I could do better. However I will find a way."

Marshall suffered so deeply after his wife's death that his doctor worried that he might have a breakdown. A general checkup revealed high blood pressure and a thyroid condition. Marshall needed a change of scenery; luckily, not long afterward, he was offered a chance to move out of Washington and the house that was filled with mementos of his wife. In November 1927 he relocated to Fort Benning, near Columbus, Georgia, to take up the post of assistant commandant at the Army Infantry School.

Marshall threw himself into his work at Benning and proved to be a brilliant teacher and academic organizer. The school had been established nine years earlier to provide training and instruction for infantry officers. Marshall saw that there was room for much improvement in what Forrest Pogue has called the strict "military scholasticism" of the school. During a field exercise outside Tientsin, Marshall had encountered a young graduate of Benning sitting on the bank of a canal trying to compose one of the standard five-paragraph field orders military men of that time were taught to write at such schools as Benning. By the time the man had finished writing, Marshall observed, the opportunity for an attack had passed. "The man was no fool," Marshall later wrote a friend, "but he had been taught an absurd system . . . and I then and there formed an intense desire to get my hands on Benning." Marshall had learned in World War I that 20th-century war was different from the warfare of the past. In modern combat, events in the field followed one another with dizzying rapidity. Military education needed to reflect that change. Marshall wanted to form a corps of officers who could think on their feet.

To help in his struggle to "expunge the bunk, complications, and ponderosities" of education at Benning, Marshall recruited some of the brightest military minds of the day. They included men he would work with later, such as Lieutenant Colonel Joseph W. Stilwell and Major Omar N. Bradley. He noted at that time that Stilwell, whom he had assigned to the tactical section, was "qualified for any command in peace or war." He remembered that judgment later when he posted Stilwell in China during World War II. Omar Bradley discovered that if Marshall believed in a man he wisely left him alone to do his work. During the entire two years Bradley spent as head of the weapons section at the Army Infantry School, Marshall visited him in his office only twice. Years later, picked for a top job in World War II, Bradley found it "astonishing" that he had been remembered from Benning. During his five years at Benning, Marshall gathered about him the band of men he would eventually rely on as chief of

Troops on review at the Fort Benning Infantry School outside Columbus, Georgia. Marshall accepted a position as assistant commander of infantry at the school in order to avoid thinking about the recent death of his wife.

I have possessed myself in patience, but I'm fast getting too old to have any future of importance in the Army.

—GEORGE MARSHALL
shortly before his 55th birthday, to Pershing

staff, jotting down their names in his "little black book." Over 200 men who were either students or faculty at the school during Marshall's tenure would serve the nation as generals in World War II.

Uncle George, as the students at Benning called Marshall — when he was out of earshot — was a very busy man. But he was also a very lonely one. He had lost weight and continued to be plagued by a thyroid problem. In the two years after Lily's death, both Marshall's mother and Lily's also passed away. He had a pleasant home on the post, "the nicest one I ever had," he later said, but when his sister, Marie, came to visit she found that each room contained a photo of Lily.

Despite his feeling of loss, Marshall did his best not to become a recluse. He had an active social life and was often invited to occasions in nearby Columbus. He was older now and no longer cut as dashing a figure as the young man who had whirled duchesses off their feet on the dance floors of London. At the age of almost 50, his plain American good looks had begun to droop around the edges. But Marshall, with his keen blue eyes and self-confident charm, was still attractive to many women. In the summer of 1929 he met one who also attracted him. Because loss of a loved one was the agony that informed his existence, he naturally turned to someone who would understand. Katherine Tupper Brown shared his sense of bereavement. Her lawyer husband had been killed a little over a year before by an angry client. When she learned of the murder, the beautiful former actress from Baltimore felt that her life was over. Her first reaction, like Marshall's, had been to get away. After traveling for many months, she came to visit a friend in Columbus.

Katherine Tupper Brown and George Catlett Marshall first met at a small cocktail party in Columbus. Katherine never forgot her first glimpse of the colonel: "George had a way of looking right straight through you," she said. Marshall, in fact, could not take his eyes off her. The two spent most of the evening talking to one another, and as it grew late, Marshall asked if he could drive her home. After

The depression Marshall felt at the death of his wife was relieved somewhat when he met Katherine Tupper Brown at a party in Baltimore in 1929. The former actress, who had also lost her spouse, liked Marshall immediately; they were married less than a year later.

asking if he knew the way to the home of her friend, Katherine agreed. Somehow, however, Marshall managed to take an extremely circuitous route to her destination. After about an hour, Katherine commented, "Colonel, you obviously don't know your way around Columbus at all." "Mrs. Brown," he answered, "I know Columbus so well it's taken me all this time to keep away from the street where you're staying."

Before Katherine would assent to marry Marshall, her three children had to approve of him. Katherine had two sons: Allen, 12, and Clifton, 14; and a daughter, Molly, who was 16. Marshall had always had a way with children, and he quickly won them over. In a letter to Pershing in 1930, he wrote delightedly that he was acquiring "a complete family." In the letter, Marshall also asked the general if he would be his best man at a wedding to take place on October 15, 1930, at the Emmanuel Episcopal Church in Baltimore.

5

Holding the Fort

Katherine and George Marshall embarked optimistically on their new life together just as the nation was entering its darkest economic hour — the Great Depression. On Black Thursday, October 24, 1929 (a year before the wedding of George and Katherine), the stock market crashed. The slide into the depths of the depression had been long and slow, but by the time Marshall's tour of duty at Fort Benning was over, in 1932, the crisis was acute. Unemployment, at 1.5 million in 1929, had risen to 13 million by the end of 1932. President Herbert Hoover's laissez-faire capitalism made worse an already sagging economy. When he finally took some initiative, it was much too little too late. Shantytowns, dubbed "Hoovervilles," sprang up like weeds across the United States, the unemployment rate soared, and millions of families went hungry. In the summer of 1932, World War I veterans marched on Washington, D.C., to demand an advance on the bonus payments that had been promised them.

My relief of mind would be tremendous if we just had too much of something besides patriotism and spirit.
—GEORGE MARSHALL
on the U.S. state of preparedness before the war

The "bonus army," a large group of disgruntled World War I veterans who had been denied benefits promised by the government, marches on Washington, D.C., in the fall of 1932. The bedraggled "army" was a symptom of the general discontent that spread through the country during the Great Depression.

With presidential elections just a few months away, the army chief of staff, Douglas MacArthur, dealt a fatal blow to Hoover's reelection campaign by using tanks and tear gas to disperse the very men who had once risked their lives overseas for the United States.

The best antidote to mental stagnation that any army officer in my position can have.
—GEORGE MARSHALL
on the CCC (Civilian Conservation Corps)

Hoover's chief Democratic opponent was the governor of New York, Franklin Delano Roosevelt. The Democratic candidate was promising a "New Deal," and desperate Americans felt that they needed and deserved one. With the bad taste of the "bonus army" incident lingering, the voters overwhelmingly elected FDR. Hoover carried only six states. A great sense of relief spread across the country when Roosevelt finally took the oath of office. In his inaugural speech, on March 4, 1933 (perhaps one of the most eagerly attended in U.S. history), he told the country that "the only thing we have to fear is fear itself. Our greatest primary task is to put people to work. This is no unsolvable problem if we face it wisely and courageously."

During his first 100 days in office, Roosevelt passed a torrent of legislation through Congress. One of his first acts, just a few weeks after being sworn in, was to establish the Civilian Conservation Corps. The CCC was originally intended to provide work, training, and quarters for 250,000 unemployed young men and boys, ages 17 to 25. Eventually 2.5 million would benefit from its programs. The young men were assigned to public projects, including reforestation programs and the construction of dams and bridges. But who could organize this program and keep the thousands who participated in it under control? Chief of Staff MacArthur suggested to President Roosevelt that the army might administer the CCC. This was a calculated act of self-preservation on the part of the chief of staff. With the country in a desperate economic situation, Congress was itching to cut military appropriations. Through the CCC, MacArthur believed, he could keep his men in uniform. To the chief of staff's satisfaction, the job was given to the U.S. Army.

When George Marshall left Fort Benning in the summer of 1932, he was given a backwater assignment at Fort Screven, outside Savannah, Georgia. Marshall was pleased nonetheless; he had command of a battalion of about 400 men. "However small," he wrote to General Pershing, "it at least keeps me away from office work and high theory." But soon the CCC project got started, and Marshall was asked what portion of his staff at Fort Screven he could spare to help train the boys for a reforestation project. "Leave my post surgeon, my commissary officer, my post-exchange officer, and my adjutant, and I will run this command with first sergeants," he answered. On June 28, 1933, Marshall left Fort Screven to take over command of Fort Moultrie, in South Carolina, where he would continue administering the work of the CCC in that state.

Because the project was not military in nature, there were some in the army who objected to it. Marshall was not one of them; he approved of the CCC program from the beginning. When a West Point graduate came to his office to complain about having to work "with a whole lot of bums" and threatened to resign, Marshall told him, "You can't resign quick enough to suit me. It suits me just fine! Now get out of here!" Marshall found the work with the CCC gratifying. Week by week he watched as the young men were transformed by the experience in the camps. All of his frustrated paternal instincts seemed to be brought out by the job. He called in a dentist to fix the boys' teeth, engaged tutors for the illiterate, and organized expeditions to Florida, where the boys learned how to swim and sail. "That was the first time those boys came to realize they weren't just nothing," remembered Katherine Marshall. The boys were learning pride in themselves and Marshall was proud of them. He called the CCC the "greatest social experiment outside Russia."

Marshall's work with the CCC was interrupted by his most disappointing assignment to date: He received word from the adjutant general that he would be assigned to the Illinois National Guard. Marshall did not want to leave the "genial and gentle" sur-

Members of the Civilian Conservation Corps (CCC) arrive at a rural work camp in 1933. The army was assigned the task of shepherding the millions of youths who comprised the CCC; Marshall was to administer CCC operations in South Carolina.

roundings of South Carolina for a desk job in the big city. Although they had just finished redecorating their house at Fort Moultrie, the Marshalls left South Carolina in October 1933 to settle in an apartment on Chicago's North Side. During the first weeks in Chicago, Mrs. Marshall noticed that her husband "had a grey, drawn look" she had never seen before. City life disagreed with him. He was also worried, again, about his prospects for promotion. Although his job in Chicago carried an increase in pay, it would be detached service; National Guard troops were not part of the regular army and working with them would not necessarily further his career. Once put to work, however, Marshall's enthusiasm returned.

The Illinois National Guard Division had been criticized for "inadequate training." It was hardly a moment for the keepers of the peace to be unprepared. The depression had caused deep civil unrest in Chicago, and with the threat of violence in the air there was pressure on the division to get into shape. Marshall had been assigned to make certain the men passed muster. He threw himself into the task of giving the Illinois Guard "a highly disciplined, hard-working, businesslike organization." But worries about his career continued to hang over him like a dark cloud. He was aware that no chief of staff could be appointed unless he had at least 4 years left to serve before enforced retirement at the age of 64. Marshall was 54 years old in 1935 and still 2 stars away from the rank that would put him in the running for that position. He wrote to Pershing, "I can but wait, grow older, and hope for a more favorable situation in Washington."

The tide in the capital finally turned in Marshall's favor when MacArthur resigned as chief of staff. Katherine Marshall had been convinced all along that MacArthur kept her husband from getting his promotion: "George had been told that MacArthur said he was the only soldier he was afraid of. Without [George] in the running, MacArthur had it clear." On October 2, 1935, Malin Craig became chief of staff. Craig was a former protégé of Pershing's, and now old Black Jack flooded Craig's office

Marshall charts maneuvers during the Illinois National Guard war games in 1936. Marshall, who had been put in charge of the Illinois guard in 1933, was unhappy with the job and city life in Chicago.

with petitions on Marshall's behalf. In September 1936, Marshall was promoted to the rank of brigadier general.

With the promotion came a new assignment. Marshall was to assume command of the Fifth Brigade of the Third Division at the Vancouver Barracks in Washington State. Marshall was delighted with both the scenic splendor and the historic interest of the new post. He and Mrs. Marshall moved into a spacious house that had been built for an Indian fighter and occupied by a "succession of Civil War celebrities." From the windows of the house they could see the snowy crown of Oregon's Mt. Hood. After the Second World War, Marshall wistfully remembered his time in Vancouver: "Those days along the rivers of the Northwest, among its magnificent mountains, and by the picturesque seashore appealed to us as a pleasant dream in comparison with the troubled days that followed."

Marshall's enjoyment of the Northwest and the thrill of having troops at his command were temporarily marred by ill health. He had to undergo a thyroid operation just a few months after he arrived. He was soon back on his feet, however, establishing new training policies for the troops and waging war on the flood of paperwork that threatened to swamp the army administration. "Every time I turn my back," he complained, "some staff officer calls on some poor devil for a report or an extra copy for some more damned papers."

Most of Marshall's time, however, was taken up by the supervision of the 35 CCC camps scattered throughout Oregon and southern Washington. Marshall believed in the therapy of fresh air, both for restless urban youths and for himself. He took great pleasure in watching his "peaceful invasion" of boys from the big cities of the Northeast stretch their legs in the forests of the Northwest. A group from Rhode Island was stationed on the shores of the Pacific near Tillamook. Their road sign read Tillamook 18 Miles. Providence R.I. 3100.

Even farther away, across the North American continent and the Atlantic Ocean, lay Europe, where once again a terrible storm was gathering. The depression hit Europe later than it hit the United States, but when it did, it hit hard. Soon the world did not seem to be as "safe for democracy" as Woodrow Wilson had hoped after World War I. It appeared to the starving and unemployed masses of Europe that the system of democratic capitalism did not have the wherewithal to cope with the growing economic crisis. Alternatives on the left and right of the political spectrum began to seem more and more appealing. Communist and Fascist parties grew in size and popularity as the people cried out for a strong government and an end to the depression.

By the time FDR took his oath of office, totalitarian regimes were already established in two of Europe's greatest nations. Benito Mussolini and the Fascists had held power in Italy since late in 1922. In January 1933, Germany threw off the last humiliating shackles of the Versailles treaty; the parliamentary government of the Weimar Republic collapsed, and Adolf Hitler's Nazi party came to power. In July 1936, civil war broke out in impoverished Spain. The Nationalists, a faction similar in its ideas and aims to Mussolini's Fascists and Hitler's Nazis, launched a revolution against the

Spanish republic. Led by Francisco Franco, the Nationalists quickly received help from Germany and Italy. The Republicans received aid from the Soviet Union and from international brigades sympathetic to their cause, while the United States, clinging to isolationist doctrine, looked on. France was sympathetic to the Republicans but remained neutral because it feared a general European war. It soon looked as though the war in Spain was becoming a contest between the forces of fascism and those of communism — a contest that had implications for all the world.

Across the Pacific, war broke out late in 1937. Early in the 1930s the increasingly aggressive Japanese had created a puppet state in the Chinese territory of Manchuria. In 1936 the Japanese government signed a pact with Hitler, the full content of which was not known to the nervous West. Concern was mounting over Japan's unmistakably warlike intentions in Asia, and the concern was justified. On July 7, 1937, after a minor incident — staged by the Japanese — at the Marco Polo Bridge

A lifetime of dedicated service in the U.S. Army was rewarded in 1936, when Marshall, at the age of 56, was promoted to brigadier general and posted in Washington State, where he and his wife enjoyed a brief respite before the outbreak of World War II.

outside Beijing, Japan launched an invasion of China. In December the Japanese brutally occupied and sacked the Chinese city of Nanking and provocatively sunk an American gunboat, the USS *Panay*, in the Yangtze River.

In this climate of crisis, Marshall was called away from his Northwest idyll to a more important job in Washington, D.C. He had been appointed chief of the War Plans Division of the War Department. No sooner had he set foot in the capital than his career, which had seemed to move so slowly for so many years, suddenly took off. On October 15, 1938, after only three months with the War Plans Division, Marshall was made deputy chief of staff of the army. He had landed the job at a critical juncture. Two weeks earlier, Hitler and Mussolini had invited French and British leaders to a conference at Munich, Germany.

While stationed at the Vancouver Barracks in Washington State, Marshall followed news of the disturbing events in Europe — especially the rise of facism and its two chief proponents, Benito Mussolini (left) and Adolf Hitler — with growing unease.

Japanese soldiers round up Chinese civilians in the streets of Shanghai. By 1937, Japanese encroachment on north China had developed into a full-scale invasion.

Hitler demanded that Czechoslovakia, an ally of France's, surrender the Sudetenland, an area that had a large German-speaking population. In return for Hitler's promise — which would soon be broken — of no further aggression on the part of Germany, the French and British conceded. They were intimidated, and so was the American public. That fall, opinion polls revealed that 43 percent of the previously isolationist public now believed the United States could not stay out of a European war.

World War I had been fought on the ground and below it, in the trenches; much of World War II would be fought high above, in the bomber and fighter planes of the warring nations. Hitler had already shown off the destructive efficiency of his air force during the Spanish civil war. In April 1937, the Condor Legion of 43 German aircraft had dropped their cargo of bombs on Guernica, Spain. At least 1,000 people were killed in the raid, and 70 percent of the buildings in the Basque town were destroyed. The world was waking up fast to the terror of a new form of warfare.

If war in Europe was inevitable, France and Britain needed time to prepare. They also needed to purchase American-made aircraft, but America still clung desperately to the dubious security of isolationism, making it politically infeasible for President Roosevelt to suggest that American factories be set up to build planes for France and Britain. The public wanted the United States to remain neutral if a conflict broke out, and the Neutrality Act of 1937 gave that wish the force of law. If a war began, neutrality did not mean supplying aircraft to one side only. The president, who knew that America would inevitably be drawn into a war in Europe, had to find another reason to advocate using government money to build the factories. At a White House conference on November 14, 1938, he proposed a program to build 10,000 planes for U.S. national defense.

After setting forth his plans, the president asked those present for their opinions. The conference was one of Marshall's first official encounters with the president, and because he did not know Roosevelt's true motives, which were to get the U.S. war machine geared up without alarming the isolationists, he found that he disagreed with him. It seemed to Marshall that FDR was only talking about machinery and foolishly forgetting the men who would man the aircraft. The president confronted Marshall and sought his approval of the plan, asking, "Don't you think so George?" Marshall was not very happy at the use of his first name, which he later called a "misrepresentation of our intimacy." He answered, "I am sorry, Mr. President, but I don't agree with that at all." Roosevelt appeared startled, but like Pershing years earlier, he was not the sort of man who was offended by the truth (although he would never call Marshall by his first name again). In the months that followed, Marshall painted for Roosevelt a dismal picture of unpreparedness throughout the U.S. armed forces, convincing the president not only of the need for more appropriations but of the caliber of the man who had answered his questions with such blunt honesty.

The U.S. war machine gears up in a Seattle, Washington factory, where huge bombers known as Flying Fortresses are under construction. The 22-ton bombers were to be sent to the aid of the beleaguered Royal Air Force of Great Britain.

In early April 1939, Marshall was summoned to the White House, where Roosevelt informed him that he would succeed General Craig as chief of staff. (Craig was set to retire in September.) Marshall wanted to make certain that they really understood one another. The president had already gotten a taste of Marshall's no-nonsense nature, but now he was warned again. "It was an interesting interview," Marshall recalled. "I told him that I wanted the right to say what I think and it would often be unpleasing. 'Is that alright?' He said, 'Yes.' I said, 'You said *yes* pleasantly, but it may be unpleasant.' "

When Marshall left the Oval Office, he was uncertain whether Roosevelt still wanted to give him the job. But Roosevelt had already made up his mind, and he would not be the last president to appreciate Marshall's forthrightness. "Truth has no qualifying adjectives," said Harry S. Truman years later. "A man either tells the truth or he doesn't. General Marshall was the exemplification of the man of truth." In the coming months Marshall would continue to tell the uncompromising truth, but it was a truth that would indeed be "unpleasing."

6
The Gathering Storm

George C. Marshall was sworn in as chief of staff on September 1, 1939, just hours after Hitler's forces invaded Poland and began World War II. The world had already witnessed Germany's betrayal of the promises it had made to Britain and France at Munich in 1938. Hitler's armies took not just the Sudetenland; by March 15, 1939, they had occupied all of Czechoslovakia. Then Hitler and his former foe, the Soviet leader Joseph Stalin, signed a non-aggression pact and between them set about dismembering Poland. Britain and France, which had pledged to help Poland in the event of an assault on that country, now kept their promise: Two days after the invasion of Poland they declared war on Germany.

My day of induction was momentous, with the starting of what appears to be a world war.
—GEORGE MARSHALL
a few days after being sworn in as chief of staff

According to army regulations, the chief of staff is the "immediate advisor of the Secretary of War" and is charged by him "with the planning, development, and execution of the military program." As Europe was overwhelmed by war, Marshall suddenly found that he had to be many things to many men.

U.S. Army chief of staff Marshall argues for compulsory military training before the Senate Military Affairs Committee in 1940. Despite the prevailing isolationist mood in the nation, Marshall was already convinced that the United States would be drawn inevitably into the war in Europe.

I am disappointed in all of you. You haven't disagreed with a single thing I have done all week.
—GEORGE MARSHALL
to his staff after his first week as chief of staff

He took part in countless meetings with the president, with cabinet members, with advisers, and with politicians of both parties. The last group was a particular problem for Marshall, who always tried to remain aloof from partisan debate and party politics. Elections were coming up in 1940, and everyone in Washington seemed to be cowed by the isolationist mood of the nation. Marshall was inclined to agree with the member of his staff who complained that U.S. politicians would "rather lose a war than lose a vote."

Franklin Delano Roosevelt was a wily, skillful politician. Marshall had already expressed his concern that informal discussions with the beguiling president "could get you into trouble." Now, as a chief of staff who saw war looming on the horizon and who realized that U.S. forces were woefully unprepared, Marshall had to learn how to get Roosevelt's ear and hold it. One of the first projects that brought Marshall into conflict with Congress and the president was a proposed program to build the army back up to the National Defense Act allowance of 280,000 men. So far, Roosevelt had only been committed to a program of building up an air force that he believed would deter aggression against the United States and its neighbors in Latin America. Marshall, watching the events in Europe, knew that a more thorough program was called for. But how could he get his message across to the president?

The way, this time, was through Secretary of the Treasury Henry Morgenthau, who came to believe in Marshall's ideas. Morgenthau arranged a meeting with Roosevelt and Marshall on May 13, 1940. Three days earlier, the German *blitzkrieg* (lightning warfare), which had already fallen upon Denmark and Norway, swept west into the Netherlands, Belgium, and Luxembourg. At the conference with Roosevelt and Marshall, Morgenthau asked the president to listen to what his chief of staff had to say. Roosevelt retorted, "I know exactly what he would say. There is no necessity for me to hear him at all." He seemed to be begging for a taste of the unpleasantness Marshall had promised him. Walking over to the chair where the president was sitting, Marshall insisted quietly but firmly on taking three minutes of his time. His wish granted, Marshall proceeded to explain the situation in his typically straightforward manner, telling Roosevelt, "If you don't do something and do it right away, I don't know what is going to happen to this country." Roosevelt asked Marshall to return the next day with a precise list of his requirements.

In late May, FDR asked Congress for defense appropriations of $1 billion. Marshall later saw this as the watershed event in the struggle toward preparedness. From this period until the American entry into the war, much of Marshall's work to convince the president and Congress of the need to spend more would be easier. Convinced of the cause he was representing, Marshall made a compelling speaker. Congressional committees seldom failed to be moved by his words. Still, the chief of staff had to move cautiously. Marshall did not want "to create the feeling that I, as leader of the military portion of affairs at that time, was trying to force the country into a lot of actions which it opposed." America was a democracy, and Marshall knew that the first move had to come from Congress and the public.

Stand right up and tell him what you think and stand right there. There are too few people who do it and he likes it.

—HENRY MORGANTHAU
U.S. secretary of state, to Marshall on how to approach President Roosevelt

And the mood in the United States was changing. The French army, reputed to be the best in Europe, was now reeling under the fury of the blitzkrieg. There could be no doubt that Hitler was a threat far greater than had been previously imagined. On June 10, 1940, Roosevelt made a speech in Charlottesville, Virginia, expressing his outrage at what was happening in Europe. Italy, a member of the Axis alliance with Germany and Japan, had invaded France earlier that day. Roosevelt knew he must begin to prepare the American people for an inevitable involvement in the war. He was taking a chance, because his Republican opponent in the upcoming elections, Wendell Willkie, would jump at any opportunity to accuse him of warmongering. Roosevelt's own campaign was based on a pledge not to send the boys into "any foreign wars." Nonetheless, in his speech at Charlottesville the president forcefully accused the isolationists of suffering from the "delusion that we of the United States can

Behaving more like tourists than an occupying army, German soldiers take a leisurely stroll through the infamous Montmartre district of Paris in the summer of 1940. The French capital had fallen to the Germans on June 15.

safely permit the United States to become a lone island, a lone island in a world dominated by the philosophy of force." Soon afterward, George Marshall echoed these sentiments. On June 12, three days before Paris fell to the Nazis, he told the 1940 graduates of his alma mater, VMI, that "the world we have known may be revolutionized" and that the "peaceful liberty we have accepted so casually may be a hazard in this ghastly game abroad."

After the French were forced to sign an armistice with Germany and Italy, the British found themselves standing alone against the Nazi war machine. British prime minister Neville Chamberlain had once said that it was "best and safest to count on nothing from the Americans but words." For the time being, this was all that Britain was to receive.

Chamberlain himself had been forced out of office after the invasion of Norway in April. The man who took his place at the head of a special wartime coalition government was Winston Churchill. Churchill believed that America would eventually come to the aid of Britain and Europe, and he promptly and eloquently set about trying to convince the United States of the role he believed it was destined to play.

In early June the British had begun evacuating the port of Dunkirk, leaving behind a defeated France. The British army also left behind much of its munitions supply, and now Churchill began a desperate plea to Roosevelt for new supplies. The prime minister wanted ships, planes, guns, and ammunition. Roosevelt wanted to give them to him,

British statesman Winston Churchill, alarmed at German aggression in western Europe and his own country's military unpreparedness, makes a public plea in April 1939 for volunteers to fill out the ranks of Britain's Home Guard.

and Marshall was all for American generosity as long as it did not cut into the budget for his army and affect America's own military buildup. But both Americans were hampered in their willingness to help the beleaguered British by the Neutrality Act, which prevented them from supplying arms to "belligerent" nations. Only items that were certified as "surplus" could be sold to the British; so it was easy enough to send machine guns and mortars to England but quite a different matter when it came to warships. In September, however, Churchill and Roosevelt found a loophole in the Neutrality Act. In return for the use of bases on British territory in Newfoundland, the Bahamas, and elsewhere, the Americans supplied the British with 50 destroyers.

In the fall of 1940, Roosevelt was elected to his third term. (It was only after Roosevelt's death, during his fourth term, that U.S. presidents were limited by law to two consecutive terms of power.) The combination of Churchill in Britain and Roosevelt in America would prove to be a fortuitous one. Soon the two were conversing regularly by transatlantic telephone. Later, the relationship that developed between them would be called "the partnership that saved the west."

In September the Selective Service Act was passed. The act made all healthy American males between the ages of 21 and 45 subject to conscription into the military. But even as the Selective Service Act was debated the British were enduring a horrific air assault by the Nazi air force, the Luftwaffe. London was bombed continuously for 69 days. Britain's industrial centers also came under attack. In November, the British ambassador in Washington announced that Britain's arsenal and finances were exhausted. They could no longer pay for what they were receiving from the United States.

In December, Roosevelt began outlining the Lend-Lease plan, a program to aid Britain and at the same time make the United States "the arsenal of democracy." The United States would lend Britain supplies on the understanding that they would be returned in kind after the war. Roosevelt compared this to lending one's neighbor a hose to put out the fire that was burning down his house. Others were skeptical; Senator Howard Taft observed that "lending war equipment is like lending chewing gum — you don't want it back." Nevertheless, the Good Samaritan approach appealed to the American public, and Lend-Lease passed through Congress in the late winter of 1941.

Although Stalin and Hitler had signed a nonaggression pact, the Nazis began air attacks on the great nation to their east on June 22, 1941. There had been warnings that a betrayal was coming, but Stalin refused to heed them. When the German ambassador came to the foreign ministry in Moscow with a declaration of war, Russian statesman Vyacheslav Molotov asked him, "Have we really deserved this?"

A democracy has a very hard time in a war, particularly at the start of a war. They can never get ready in advance. The conditions are such that they are susceptible to surprise action, and an arbitrary government like the Hitler government has every advantage in these respects.
—GEORGE MARSHALL

The British knew that he was not out to make American points or British points, but trying to win the war the best way. The Congress knew he was talking to them straight with no politics involved.

—TOM HANDY
U.S. general, on Marshall

Neither Churchill nor Roosevelt had illusions about the nature of Stalin's regime. Even then political purges were going on that would eventually take the lives of millions of Russians. Nevertheless, after Germany attacked the Soviet Union, Churchill marched into the House of Commons and declared that he would come to the aid of the Devil himself if only the Devil would fight Hitler, and the United States promised the Russians a billion dollars' worth of supplies under the Lend-Lease program. The Allies were overjoyed at Russia's entry into the war. They hoped they would be able to supply the arms and watch as the great Bolshevik and Nazi armies bled one another dry.

While Marshall was fighting for munitions and public support for the army, he also had to begin selecting men who were capable of leading it. The officer corps had to be expanded. Promotions moved slowly in the military, as Marshall was painfully aware through personal experience. Seniority was the main criterion climbing up the ranks, but by the time a man made it to the top, he was often too old and unfit for the rigors of warfare. Marshall convinced Congress to reform the system of promotions to allow the temporary advancement "in time of war or national emergency" of men of the chief of staff's and secretary of war's choosing. Out came the little black book, and men like Eisenhower and Patton leapfrogged over the heads of their superiors — but not without first being put to the "severest tests" that Marshall could devise in time of peace. "I was accused," Marshall said, "of getting rid of all the brains in the Army. I couldn't reply that I was eliminating considerable arteriosclerosis."

In Washington, Marshall received an education in the political impediments to gearing up for war in a democratic nation. Complicated procedures and layers of government bureaucracy seemed to make simple tasks difficult, but Marshall understood that such hurdles were in place to protect the constitutional rights of military personnel, that becoming a soldier should not mean giving up one's rights as a U.S. citizen. One historian who heard Marshall speak on his program for the army noted with pleasure, "If he represents our Army, the American Army is yet a part of the American people. He pointed out the time consumed by working in a democracy, but with no impatience. He evidently thinks the advantages are worth the time."

American troops, Marshall believed, should be treated like voting adults, like citizens, not disciplined without explanation like children. No matter how busy he and his staff were, they would always be attentive to complaints from recruits, whether about rotten eggs in the canteen, an epidemic of the flu, or a lack of blankets or heaters. Civilian conscripts had to be treated with respect and kept informed about the war. Questions sent to him by Mrs. Roosevelt about the treatment of black troops had to be answered within 24 hours. Marshall set up an educational program run by army commanders. His men were not to be blind cannon fodder. They had to understand what the war was about. He approached Hollywood filmmaker Frank Capra and asked him to make a series of documentaries called *Why We Fight*. Capra, who had directed the famous feature films *It Happened One Night* and

Hollywood filmmaker Frank Capra (right) consults Major Hugh Stewart (left) of the U.S. Army Film Unit during the production of the first of a series of Allied propaganda movies entitled *Why We Fight*. Marshall personally recruited Capra for the job.

A rescue boat searches for survivors while the USS *Tennessee* burns in Pearl Harbor following the Japanese surprise attack on December 7, 1941. (Note the two sailors in the superstructure of the *Tennessee*.)

Mr. Deeds Goes to Town, said that he had never made a documentary before. "Capra," Marshall replied amicably, "I have never been Chief of Staff before."

The best way I can express it is to tell you that I want George to be the Pershing of the Second World War—and he cannot be that if we keep him there.

—FRANKLIN DELANO ROOSEVELT
to Pershing on why he wanted to give Marshall command of Operation Overlord

Meanwhile, another country was watching Russia's entry into the war with great satisfaction. Now that Russian troops would be tied up fighting Hitler in the west, the Japanese could aggressively pursue their own goals in the Pacific. Deeply suspicious of the Japanese, Marshall had sent MacArthur $10 million to build up the U.S. defenses in the Philippines, and by late November 1941, there were indications that the Japanese were about to make another move in the Pacific. The Americans believed the most likely target was the Philippines. But in Tokyo, General Yamamoto had already decided that Japan could not win a war in the Pacific unless the U.S. fleet in Hawaiian waters was destroyed.

The series of errors and misunderstandings that led to the destruction of the American fleet at Pearl Harbor would be almost comic had the result not been the loss of 2,403 American lives, 6 battleships, and 149 planes. The Americans knew something was coming. Cryptographers had broken the Japanese code. MacArthur was notified and put his forces in the Philippines on war alert. The chief of naval operations, Admiral Stark, did not believe the Japanese fleet that had moved out into the Pacific was headed for Hawaii. Nonetheless, he ordered General Short, at Pearl Harbor, to put his troops on war alert. Because of a discrepancy between codes for levels of preparedness used in Washington and Hawaii, however, the message was not interpreted correctly. On Sunday morning, December 7, word was received in Washington that Japan was breaking off relations with the United States as of 1:00 P.M. that day. New messages were sent off by telegraph to the bases in the Pacific, but the Western Union messenger bearing the one intended for General Short did not peddle his bike up to the base on Oahu until six hours after the waves of Japanese bombers had circled away from the smoking ruins of the American fleet and back out over the Pacific.

7
The Big One

War in a democracy is no bed of roses.
—GEORGE MARSHALL
to Dwight Eisenhower

On December 8, 1941, the day after the Japanese surprise attack on Pearl Harbor, the United States declared war on Japan. On December 11, Japan's allies, Germany and Italy, declared war on the United States. The isolationists were silent now, and America's military leaders were faced with the task of mobilizing their forces and winning what would come to be known as "the big one," World War II.

Who were the men Marshall would be working with throughout the war? Marshall was immediately responsible to the secretary of war, Henry L. Stimson. Stimson was 72 when he took the job, but despite the age difference between them, Stimson and Marshall found that they were extremely compatible. Their offices were next to one another and connected by a door that was seldom closed. Like Marshall, Stimson was uninterested in partisan politics. But the secretary of war, a former lawyer, did know how to handle politicians — including the president. Stimson, Marshall gratefully noted after the war, kept "the politicians off me."

Admiral Ernest King, commander in chief of the U.S. fleet, General H. H. Arnold, commander in chief of the U.S. Army Air Corps, and General George C. Marshall, U.S. Army chief of staff (left to right) on their way to a meeting with President Roosevelt. It was as army chief of staff during World War II that Marshall would fulfill his potential as a leader and administrator.

Admiral William D. Leahy was chosen personally by Roosevelt as head of the Joint Chiefs of Staff. The new job had been created especially for Leahy, and he acted adeptly as a kind of go-between for the chiefs of staff and the president. The other members of the Joint Chiefs of Staff were Admiral Ernest J. King, commander of the U.S. Navy; General Henry ("Hap") Arnold, commander of the Army Air Corps; and of course General George C. Marshall, commander of the army.

The interservice rivalry between army and navy in the United States has always been strong, and sometimes even bitter. The Joint Chiefs of Staff were set up so that a delicate balance of two army generals and two navy admirals was established. But the balance was tilted somewhat because the commander in chief, President Roosevelt, was a navy man. Admiral King, therefore, never had to fight as hard for what he requested for the navy as Marshall did when asking for army appropriations.

Two of the most formidable weapons of the U.S. Air Force during World War II — the massive B-24 bomber and two P-40 fighters painted to look like sharks. The fighters would soon engage Japanese Zeros in dogfights over the Pacific.

Marshall (left) confers with Secretary of War Henry L. Stimson. Marshall's administrative genius combined with Stimson's shrewd political sense made them the ideal duo to run the U.S. war effort.

Marshall, however, had no intention of accepting the situation without offering some resistance. At one meeting, where Roosevelt seemed to grant the navy every wish, Marshall asked the president if he could at least stop "speaking of the Army as 'they' and the Navy as 'us.' "

It was perhaps fortuitous that the navy was given preference at the start, because the war America entered was at the outset a naval one. Luckily, all the aircraft carriers based at Pearl Harbor had been out at sea when the Japanese struck, and many of the ships that were sunk or damaged in the harbor were later salvaged. Nonetheless, the war in the Pacific did not go well at first. By the end of January 1942, the Japanese had landed on the northern- and southernmost islands of the Philippines, seized the islands of Wake and Guam, and launched offensives on Hong Kong, British Borneo, and Burma. They held much of Thailand and Malaysia and continued the offensive in China by seizing the international concessions in Shanghai. After making a brave stand on the Bataan Peninsula, General MacArthur and his troops were forced to withdraw from the Philippines. In his famous parting words, MacArthur vowed, "I shall return," but the situation looked grim for the Allies in the Pacific.

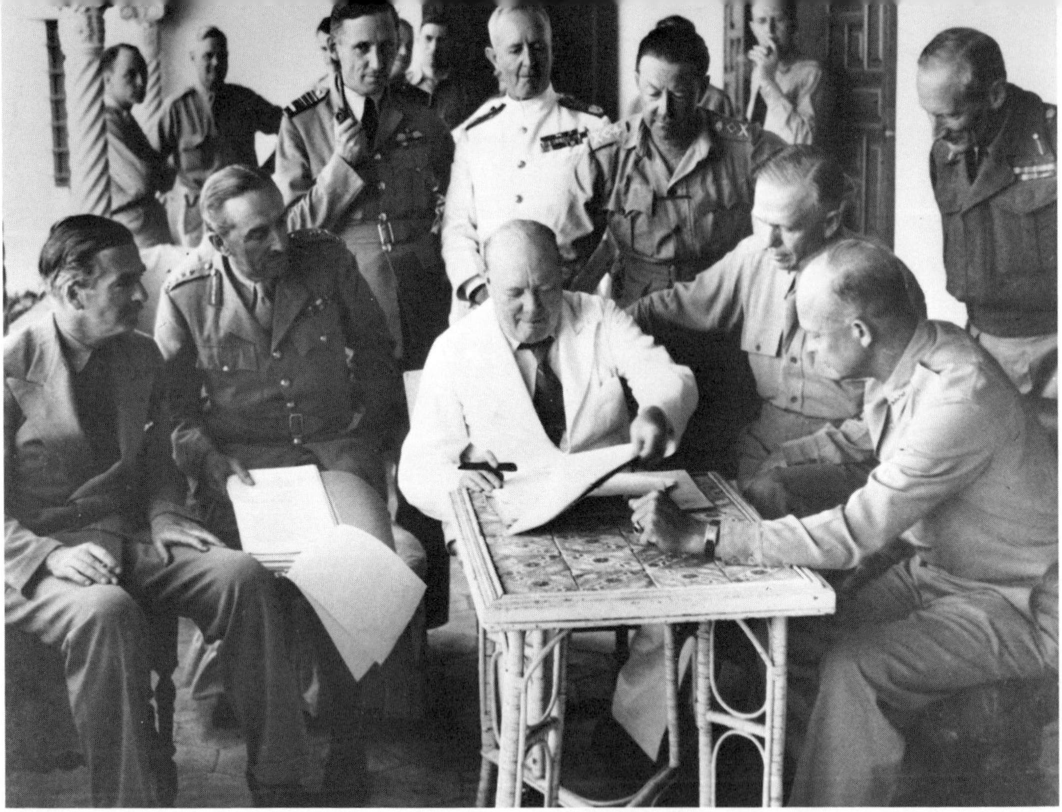

Allied military leaders plan the invasion of French North Africa in 1942. Surrounding British prime minister Churchill are (left to right) British foreign secretary Anthony Eden, British general Sir Alan Brooke, British air chief marshal Sir Arthur Tedder, British admiral Sir Andrew B. Cunningham, British general Sir Harold Alexander, U.S. generals Marshall and Eisenhower, and British general Sir Bernard Montgomery.

Admiral King was under instructions that the war in the Atlantic was the first priority, but it must have been difficult to exercise restraint while the islands of the Pacific were being swallowed up by the Japanese juggernaut. In the meantime, the operation that was being secretly planned was an Allied landing in North Africa. The British had been fighting in Libya and Egypt since early in the war. Against the Italians they had been successful, but then the Germans joined the struggle. Under the leadership of the "Desert Fox," the brilliant field-commander Erwin J. E. Rommel, the German panzer tanks had forced the British back into Egypt. Marshall was unhappy with the scheme for invading North Africa. He wanted to send troops across the English Channel into northern France first. But Roosevelt and the British insisted that the invasion of Europe must be preceded by the establishment of a base in Africa, and Marshall had no choice but to follow the orders of the commander in chief.

The Allied landing on the Moroccan beaches went better than expected. On the evening of November 8, 1942, at a football game in Washington, Katherine Marshall learned why her husband had been detained at the office. The game was interrupted by the announcement that an expeditionary force had successfully landed on the African coast. "The football players turned somersaults and handsprings down the center of the field: the crowd went wild," Mrs. Marshall recalled. "We had struck back." American troops were still inexperienced, however, and that inexperience showed in Africa, causing the British to compose a rueful song, "How Green was My Ally." But by the summer of 1943, the American troops were battle hardened and the Germans were on the run across the deserts of North Africa.

Now, Marshall trusted, the British and Americans could agree to set an invasion of Europe in motion. He hoped that he would be able to lead that operation himself. This was the one honor he coveted. Although he was now receiving the public recognition he so justly deserved — he would be named Man of the Year by *Time* magazine for 1943 and was being talked about as a potential presidential candidate — such accolades meant nothing to him. When a bill came before Congress proposing to promote him to the highest rank the U.S. Army had to give — five-star general — he laughingly dismissed it, claiming he would not be able to stand being referred to as "Field Marshal Marshall." All he desired was to be allowed to do for his country what Pershing had done in World War I — lead the troops of liberation into Europe.

The tide was turning in favor of the Allies. The Germans were being routed from North Africa, and surging U.S. naval might had turned back the Japanese fleet in the Pacific. Churchill and Roosevelt were planning a combined British-American assault on Italy. At first Roosevelt wanted to make Marshall supreme commander of the American forces that would invade Europe, as Pershing had been in World War I. But there was no one else Roosevelt felt he could rely on as chief of staff the way he relied on Marshall. Roosevelt asked Marshall if he wanted the job. Although Marshall wanted it desperately, he insisted that Roosevelt make the decision he believed was in the best interest of the country. That settled it. Roosevelt wanted and needed Marshall in the capital. "I didn't feel I could sleep at ease if you were out of Washington," the president told the chief of staff.

Marshall remained in Washington. Although he was a disappointed man, he tried hard not to show it. And Roosevelt's assessment of him was correct. That winter *Time* magazine would hail Marshall as the "indispensable man" and a "trustee for the nation." The decision to stay on in Washington *was* in the best interest of the country. No one could handle the running of a global war the way Marshall did. Every morning at nine he arrived in his office, and staff members who had worked through the wee hours gave him a full picture of all theaters of war. "It went off just like a theatrical thing," Marshall said of those morning presentations. "You saw the whole war up to the last minute — done in such a way that it was easy, in a sense, to comprehend."

Marshall takes an after-dinner ride on his sorrel, Prepared. Running a war on a global scale was a nerve-racking and exhausting task; the army chief of staff's favorite method of relaxation was horseback riding.

Every evening a car picked up the chief of staff and carried him home to Fort Meyers — where he made a point of getting to bed early. Marshall knew that his health depended on discipline, self-control, and regular exercise. He tried to keep a tight rein on his temper as well, knowing that when it got hot he was the one most likely to get burned. He told his wife, "I cannot allow myself to get angry. That would be fatal. It's too exhausting." Another effective way of dealing with the stress was to take an early morning gallop on his sorrel, Prepared, often accompanied by his goddaughter, Rose Page, or his stepdaughter, Molly.

The invasion of Italy went as planned. By June 4, 1944, Allied troops had fought their way to Rome, driving the stubborn Nazis before them. But among the many losses on the road to Rome was one that affected General Marshall deeply: His beloved stepson Allen was killed by a German sniper's bullet. Three weeks after his death, Marshall visited the site where Allen had been shot. He found his stepson's grave among 7,000 others at the Anzio beachhead where Allied troops had been landing since January. Marshall had always been aware of the personal tragedy of war, and had tried to impress it on others, including President Roosevelt. Working a desk job in the war made it all too easy to become hardened and forget that the casualty reports represented individual lives. Through personal contact with the troops, Marshall tried to prevent himself from becoming too abstract in his perception of the horrors of war; no man was more acutely conscious of those horrors than Marshall as he knelt before the modest marker over his stepson's fresh grave at Anzio.

If I had to name the six greatest Americans of the 20th century, I would certainly include George Marshall.
—CLEMENT ATTLEE
British prime minister

June 6, 1944, would go down in history as D day. General Eisenhower, who had proven himself in command of the U.S. forces in North Africa, was given the honor of leading the American troops in the invasion of Normandy, France. At first the invasion was postponed because of bad weather, but when the rain and wind continued, the Allied troops forged ahead anyway. "I think we have these Huns at the top of the toboggan slide," Marshall wrote to

U.S. soldiers swarm off amphibious troop carriers and onto the beach at Normandy, France, on D day, June 6, 1944. Marshall had hoped to lead the Allied invasion of France, but Roosevelt felt that the chief of staff would serve his country better by remaining in Washington to oversee the global effort.

Roosevelt a week later, after visiting the beachhead at Normandy, "and the full crash of the Russian offensive should put the skids under them." The Germans put up a desperate fight, but in August another Allied force landed in the south of France and the two armies began closing the pincers on Paris, where the underground French Resistance, aware that liberation was on its way, began an uprising. On August 25, 1944, Allied troops liberated the city of Paris.

Even as the Germans retreated back over the Rhine, they continued their methodical execution of the Jews. Hitler wanted his goal of exterminating the Jews of Europe accomplished by the end of 1944. Eventually, over 6 million Jews were murdered. Communists, socialists, Resistance fighters, gypsies, and homosexuals were also sent to their death in German concentration camps. As the Germans conducted their murderous retreat, Allied bombers crossed the Channel nightly to pound the German cities. Berlin, Frankfurt, Dresden, and other German cities were engulfed by fire storms. Over 300,000 German civilians were killed in the Allied bombing raids.

On April 12, 1945, President Roosevelt died. He had appeared ill during his 1944 election campaign, but no one expected the end to come so suddenly. Upon hearing of the president's death that evening, Marshall drove quickly to the White House, where Mrs. Roosevelt asked him to take care of the funeral arrangements. A funeral train was sent to Georgia for the body, and as it headed back to Washington, its route was lined with thousands of stunned mourners. The next day, the man who had been president for 12 years and 1 month was buried at his family estate, in Hyde Park, New York.

Harry Truman, the former senator, had been Roosevelt's running mate in the 1944 campaign, and now, suddenly, he was the president of a country at war. Truman felt as though "the stars and all the planets" had fallen on him. He told the press, "If you fellows ever pray, pray for me." The new president had to be briefed immediately by the chiefs of staff. Despite his self-deprecation, he was a clever enough man to grasp the situation quickly. In Marshall and the others at the War Department, Truman was fortunate to inherit a staff he could count on until he could get his own footing.

Mourners line the way of President Roosevelt's funeral procession as it moves down Washington's 15th Street before turning onto Pennsylvania Avenue and heading back toward the White House, April 1945.

By late April the Allied troops were approaching the capital city of the German Reich. The goal of the British and American soldiers was to "beat the Bolsheviks to Berlin." Both the British Twenty-first Army under Field Marshal Bernard Montgomery and the U.S. Ninth Army under Lieutenant General William H. Simpson believed they could do it. But Simpson, who had the better chance, was held back by the supreme commander in Europe, Dwight D. Eisenhower, who wanted to keep his troops away from the Russians. The Germans knew which occupying army they preferred. Fearing the wrath of the approaching Soviet force, 100,000 German soldiers crossed the river Elbe to surrender to the Americans, who had halted their advance there. As the Russians entered the city, Hitler and his wife, Eva, hidden away in his bunker, committed suicide. A week later, the war in Europe was over. On May 7, 1945, the Germans signed an instrument of unconditional surrender.

A Russian soldier hoists a Soviet army victory banner over the Reichstag in Berlin, May 2, 1945. Three days later, German admiral Hans G. Friedeberg officially surrendered all German troops to the Allied generals, and the war in Europe was over.

U.S. and Soviet soldiers, representing the two prongs of the great Allied pincer that had closed on Germany and the Third Reich, finally come together on a wrecked bridge spanning the river Elbe at Torgau, Germany, in April 1945.

That same evening, Katherine Marshall found her husband strangely quiet when he returned home. Was he worried about the battle for the Pacific that lay ahead or merely exhausted? He was a 64-year-old man who for the last 6 years had uncomplainingly shouldered the sorrows and worries of a nation at war. Was the strain showing at last? Katherine Marshall did not learn until later that the general was silent because he was deeply moved. That afternoon, his close friend, Secretary of War Stimson, had paid him a touching tribute. The older man had gathered a group of generals and officials in the office of Marshall's secretary. "I want to acknowledge my great personal debt to you," Stimson told Marshall. After more warm words of praise and affection, Stimson concluded, "I have seen a great many soldiers in my lifetime, and you, sir, are the finest soldier I have ever known."

8

A Brave New World

In a war unparalleled in magnitude and horror, millions of Americans gave their country outstanding service. General George C. Marshall gave it victory.

—HARRY TRUMAN
U.S. president

No sooner had the "stars and planets" fallen on Harry S. Truman's head than he was faced with one of the most momentous decisions in the history of mankind. The first atomic bomb was successfully exploded in the desert at Alamogordo, New Mexico, in the summer of 1945. The Allies scarcely realized the degree of destructive force that they now held in their hands. Was the new weapon so much worse than the "conventional" bombs that had killed an estimated 45,000 during the 3-day Allied air attack on Dresden, Germany? Should they use this new device against their enemies?

Marshall and Stimson were in favor of the use of the bomb from the start. The alternative was an invasion of mainland Japan, and the battle for the island of Okinawa had shown how bitter that would be. The Japanese were desperate and ready to fight to the death according to their code of honor. "We had to end the war; we had to save American lives; we had to halt this terrific expenditure of money which was reaching a stupendous total," Marshall said later. "The bomb stopped the war. Therefore, it was justifiable."

Marshall was 65 years old when World War II ended, and although his mind was as clear and his posture as erect as ever, he was quite ready to retire to his Virginia estate with his wife. Katherine was soon to learn, however, that history was not yet finished with her husband.

Stimson and Marshall convinced the new president that the question was not whether to drop the bomb, but where, and when. The answer to the last question was "as soon as possible," and after reviewing a list of Japanese cities and vetoing Kyoto because of its ancient shrines and monuments, Hiroshima was chosen as the target. Truman gave the go-ahead while at the Allied conference in Potsdam, Germany. The atomic bomb was dropped on Hiroshima on August 6, 1945. In Washington, the War Department waited anxiously to hear the Japanese reaction, which they hoped would be unconditional surrender. "What we did not take into account," Marshall later recalled, "was that the destruction would be so complete, that it would be an appreciable time before the actual facts got to Tokyo. . . . There was no communication at least for a day, I think, and maybe longer." In the meantime, Marshall and Stimson grew nervous that the shock of Hiroshima would not be enough. The decision was made to drop a second bomb — the only other one the United States possessed at the time — on Nagasaki. Marshall hoped that the move would lead the Japanese, unaware that the United States had only two bombs, to think that Tokyo would be the next target. The second bomb was dropped on August 9, and Nagasaki was annihilated. The Japanese government capitulated on August 14, 1945.

There has grown in my breast through all these years of mental exertion a respect and admiration for your courage and massive strength which has been a real comfort to your fellow toilers, of whom I hope it will always be recorded that I was one.

—WINSTON CHURCHILL
British prime minister, in a letter to Marshall after V-E Day

The war was over, and Marshall was eager to retire to Dodona Manor, his home in Virginia. A week after the Japanese surrender, he addressed a letter of resignation to President Truman in which he suggested General Eisenhower be named his successor. Truman accepted his resignation and his suggestion. Now the words of praise uttered in Marshall's name were lavish. Churchill wrote to him and confided that he knew how deeply Marshall had regretted not being able to lead the Allied invasion of Europe. "It has not fallen to your lot to command the great armies," wrote the British prime minister. "You have had to create them, organize them, and inspire them."

On November 26, Marshall received a second oakleaf cluster to add to the Distinguished Service

After placing their sacred samurai swords on the table before them, Japanese generals sign documents of surrender while U.S. rear admiral F. E. M. Whiting looks on.

Cross he had been awarded for his efforts in World War I. As Marshall received the honor that marked his departure from the War Department, his words revealed that he was still thinking globally and that even as he went into retirement he was looking into the future. In his speech to the men and women assembled in the courtyard of the Pentagon that day, he said, "Most of you know how different, how fortunate is America compared with the rest of the world. . . . Today this nation with good faith and sincerity, I am certain, desires to take the lead in the measures necessary to avoid another world catastrophe, such as you have just endured. And the world of suffering people looks to us for such leadership."

"Hallelujah! Hallelujah!" hummed Katherine Marshall as she and her husband drove through the gates of Dodona Manor a few days later. How was she to know that the general's first "retirement" would be over in a matter of days? As she went upstairs to take her nap, she heard the telephone ring. Marshall answered it; he was brief and monosyllabic. Later, Katherine woke up to hear an announcement on the radio: President Truman had made Marshall his special ambassador to China. He

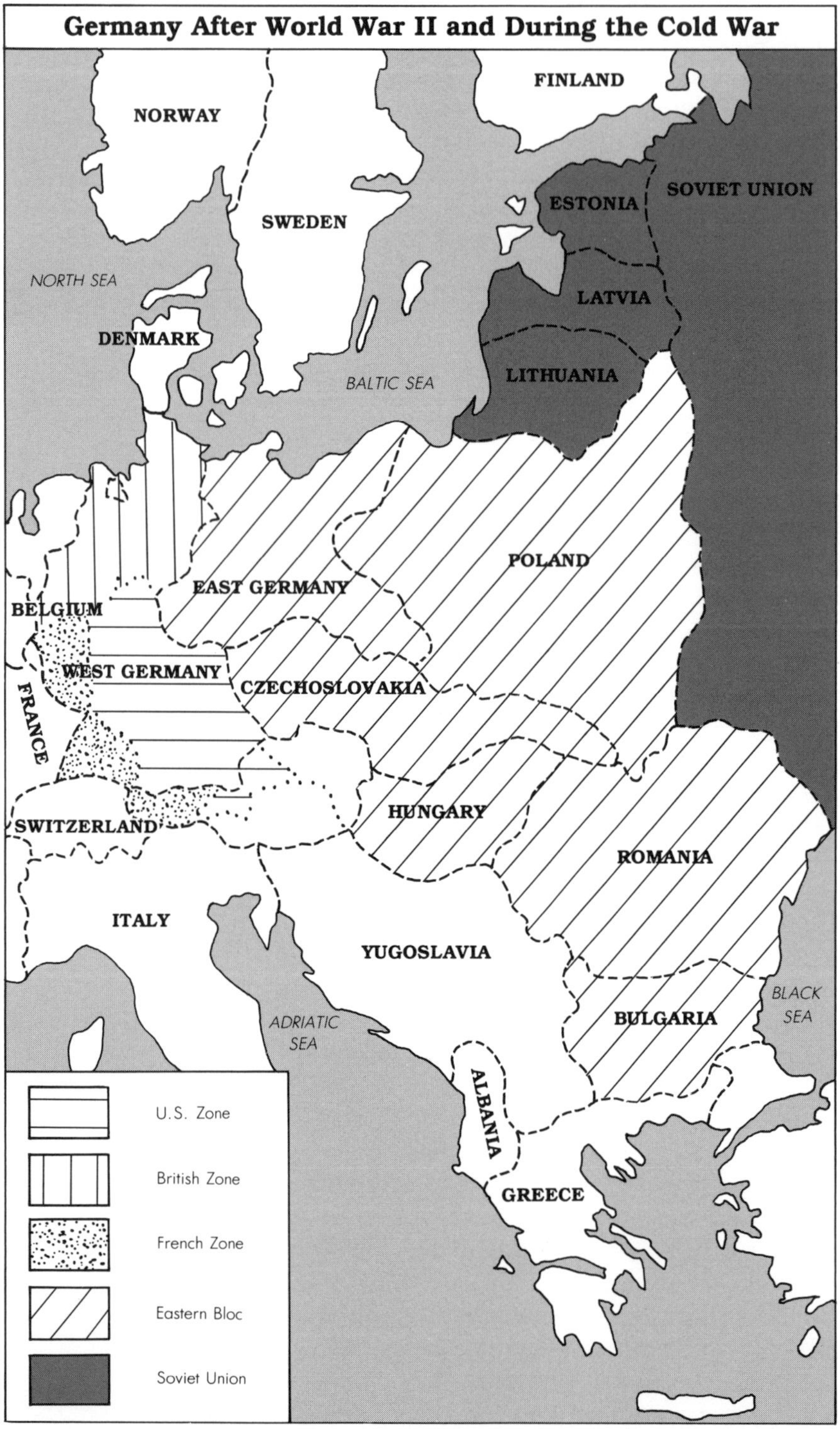
Germany After World War II and During the Cold War
FINLAND
NORWAY
SWEDEN
ESTONIA
SOVIET UNION
NORTH SEA
LATVIA
DENMARK
BALTIC SEA
LITHUANIA
POLAND
EAST GERMANY
BELGIUM
WEST GERMANY
CZECHOSLOVAKIA
FRANCE
HUNGARY
SWITZERLAND
ROMANIA
ITALY
YUGOSLAVIA
BLACK SEA
ADRIATIC SEA
BULGARIA
ALBANIA
GREECE
U.S. Zone
British Zone
French Zone
Eastern Bloc
Soviet Union

was to leave immediately. (President Truman, for his part, had been somewhat bewildered by the abrupt conversation with Marshall; after he asked the general, "Will you go to China for me?" Marshall had merely answered yes and then replaced the receiver.) When Katherine asked her husband why he had not awakened her to tell her the news, he replied, "I could not bear to tell you until you had had your rest."

In China, the more things changed, the more they seemed to stay the same. Cooperation between the rival leaders Chiang Kai-shek and Mao Zedong against the Japanese had been on-again, off-again. The conflict between the Nationalists and Communists, which had been nascent during Marshall's first assignment in China in the 1920s, had persisted throughout the war. Both sides wanted to conserve their troops for the showdown over the control of China that they knew would follow the war against Japan. By 1941, after Nationalist forces had murdered 9,000 Communist troops south of the Huang He River, all pretense at a united front against the Japanese had vanished. The Americans, however, kept trying to bring the two foes together. After the war, the United States wanted Chiang and Mao to form a coalition government. But the old rivals seemed to be right back where they had started: at one another's throat.

The mission Marshall was sent to China to accomplish was doomed to fail. The idea that Mao and Chiang could sit down together and straighten out their problems was born of an American naïveté about the situation in China. Months of shuttling back and forth between Communist headquarters in the north and Chiang's in Nanking were fruitless. The mission would be one of the only failures in General Marshall's career, and although it is doubtful that anyone else could have done a better job, it led to the myth that America had somehow "lost" China to the Communists.

Truman was beginning to recognize what the cost of wartime cooperation with the Soviets would be. Half of Europe lay under Soviet control, and Stalin soon began putting noncommunist politicians in

President Harry Truman (left) shakes hands with retired chief of staff George Marshall after adding an oakleaf cluster to Marshall's Distinguished Service Cross — one of the U.S. military's highest honors — at ceremonies held in the Pentagon court in January 1947.

A People's Liberation Army transport truck, bearing the images of Chinese Communist leaders Mao Zedong (left) and Zhou Enlai, rolls into Shanghai, recently abandoned by the vanquished Nationalist forces of Chiang Kai-shek. Marshall's attempts to negotiate a treaty between the two warring factions had failed.

Eastern Europe on trial for "terrorism." By early 1946, Truman was determined not to "play compromise" with the Soviets any longer. That spring he invited Churchill to make a speech at Fulton University. Churchill was no longer prime minister, but he was still convinced that Stalin was the Devil's not-so-distant cousin. "From Stettin in the Baltic to Trieste in the Adriatic, an iron curtain has descended across the continent," said Churchill in his speech. The cold war had begun.

Truman began pressing Marshall to give up and come home from China. He dispatched Eisenhower to China to ask Marshall how he felt about becoming secretary of state. On January 21, 1947, two weeks after arriving home from China, Marshall was sworn in as secretary of state. It was his first civilian job, and his friend Stimson, who had once held it, warned him that it was not an easy one. In his new position, his focus would quickly shift away from China and toward Europe, where the economic and political situation was increasingly desperate. The entire basis of the prewar economic system was gone. National boundaries had changed, the old order had been swept away, and millions of refugees drifted from place to place.

On March 12, 1947, the president went before a joint session of Congress to expound what would come to be known as the Truman Doctrine. Marshall was in Moscow when Truman began the speech that was sure to incense his Soviet hosts. "I believe that it must be the policy of the United States to support free peoples who are resisting attempted subjugation by armed minorities or outside pressure," said the president. "We must assist free peoples to work out their destinies in their own way."

The issue at hand was the occupation of West Germany. After the war, the country had been divided into four zones under British, French, American, and Soviet administration. The city of Berlin, in the middle of the Soviet zone, was itself divided into four sectors, each run by one of the wartime allies. The assumption was that one day it would again be the capital of a united Germany. The questions to be discussed in Moscow included the reparations payments that Moscow had forced on its zone of Germany and on Austria, which it occupied. Marshall and the British argued that although industry should be supervised to ensure that Germany was not rearming, the country's economic engine should not be dismantled but refueled and set back into motion. This was essential to the economic restoration of the European continent. But as Marshall flew back to Washington, he began to suspect that the Russians had different plans. "He came to the conclusion," his adviser and translator Charles Bohlen recalled, "that Stalin, looking over Europe, saw the best way to advance Soviet interests was to let matters drift. Economic conditions were bad. Europe was recovering slowly from the war. . . . This was the kind of crisis that Communism thrived on." Throughout the flight, Bohlen remembered, Marshall talked about finding a way to prevent the complete economic breakdown of Europe, and thus, high above the Atlantic, was formed the idea for the Marshall Plan.

The Marshall Plan, and the European Recovery Program, which was instituted by Britain and the other non-Communist Western European nations, went into effect in July 1948 and economically reinforced the political division of Eastern and Western Europe into two camps. The program was offered to all of Europe and to the Soviet Union, but Stalin decided not to participate and prevented his satellite countries from doing so. Germany would be included in the European Recovery Program — or at least the three sectors that were controlled by the West would be. The currency that was in use in all the German zones was so devalued that it was of no practical use. A currency reform was proposed, but the Soviets turned it down. The Western powers decided to act alone and introduced the deutsche mark in their zones in June.

The Russian response was immediate: They instituted their own currency reform and accused the Western powers of creating a separate West German state. They wanted their currency to be the only one used in all four sections of Berlin. When the Western powers refused to comply, the Soviets blockaded the

President Truman looks on as retiring secretary of state James Byrnes congratulates newly sworn-in secretary of state George Marshall in Washington, D.C., January 21, 1947.

German children wave to a U.S. transport plane bringing food and other vital supplies to the city of Berlin, isolated by a Soviet blockade in 1948. The blockade and subsequent airlift were the first skirmishes between East and West in what came to be known as the cold war.

city, which was an extremely vulnerable island in the center of the Soviet zone. The West responded with the Berlin airlift, which kept the city supplied throughout the long year that followed. The Berlin blockade and airlift made the division of Germany permanent and dramatically escalated tensions between the West and the Soviet Union. By March 1949, the new political, economic, and strategic order in Europe had been formalized by the signing of the North Atlantic Treaty by Britain, the United States, and the 10 other nations that would comprise NATO, the North Atlantic Treaty Organization.

At the beginning of December 1948, Marshall had been admitted to a hospital for an operation to remove his right kidney. His recovery was slow. As he convalesced at Dodona Manor, he made the decision he had been thinking about for months and wrote to Truman to say that he had decided to resign. Katherine and George Marshall left Virginia soon afterward for an extended vacation in Puerto Rico, Florida, and New Orleans.

Marshall was not the kind of man who could relax for long, however, and soon after returning to Dodona Manor, he found himself at the head of the International Red Cross. But Truman was used to counting on Marshall's steady nonpartisan advice and participation in his administration, and a new crisis was brewing in Asia. In 1949 the Communists finally achieved victory in China and drove Chiang and his Nationalists onto the island of Taiwan. That summer, the People's Republic of China was proclaimed. On June 25, 1950, Communist North Korea launched an attack on the nominally democratic Republic of Korea in the south. On June 27, Truman said that the United States would come to the aid of South Korea. In a situation that threatened to escalate into a third world war, Truman needed someone he could rely on. He had to convince Marshall that his country needed him — a call to duty that Marshall always heeded.

By the time Marshall was confirmed by the Senate as secretary of defense, the United States and a multinational group of UN troops had entered the Korean War. Marshall was familiar with the situation in Korea. The country had been occupied by the Japanese since 1910, and it had been decided during World War II that it should be given independence after the defeat of Japan. At the end of the war Marshall had helped designate the 38th parallel as the boundary between the Soviet- and Western-occupied zones. Those zones were to be temporary pending nationwide elections overseen by the United Nations. But the Soviets would not allow the UN observation team into the north for the elections. Subsequently, two states were established, a Communist regime in the north under Kim Il Sung and an authoritarian regime under Syngman Rhee in the south.

The objective of the UN forces at the outset of the Korean War was to throw the North Koreans back beyond the 38th parallel. General Douglas MacArthur had been called upon to lead the effort. MacArthur's force quickly pushed the North Koreans into retreat across the 38th parallel. But MacArthur wanted to pursue them into the north,

Friend of truth: of soul sincere,
In action faithful, and in honour clear;
Who broke no promise, serv'd no private end,
Who gained no title and lost no friend

—Lines by Alexander Pope which were sent to Marshall at the end of the war by the British chiefs of staff right up to the Yalu River along the Chinese border, with the goal of uniting Korea. Despite Communist Chinese objections, MacArthur was given the go-ahead, but Marshall secretly instructed him not to use U.S. troops in the north. That, he suspected, would provoke the Chinese. In defiance of Marshall's orders, MacArthur pushed ahead with American units.

The American public was as eager as MacArthur to strike back at the Communists, who seemed to have gobbled up so much of the world since the end of World War II. Perhaps the Korean War would provide a chance to regain China. MacArthur said that he was ready to use the atom bomb to achieve his objectives in Asia. But in November 1950, the Communist Chinese, led by Lin Biao, struck back and together with the North Koreans drove the UN forces under MacArthur all the way to the bottom of the Korean peninsula. MacArthur was allowed to counterattack and drive the Communists back to the 38th parallel again, but no farther. "Forget It: The President Wants Out" was the cable he received after begging to be allowed to go on. But MacArthur could not just "forget it," and he told the press about his frustrations. Truman instructed Marshall to write an order relieving MacArthur of his command. Although the decision was Truman's, MacArthur was paranoid about Marshall and convinced that he had been gunning for him for years. "Marshall pulled the trigger," he said.

Cadets at the Valley Forge Military Academy in Pennsylvania stand at attention for one of America's most distinguished soldiers, George C. Marshall. Marshall received many honors during his final years, the greatest of which was the Nobel Peace Prize.

When MacArthur was "shot at," he returned the round. Back in Washington a congressional hearing began on the situation in the Far East and the recall of MacArthur. MacArthur attempted to use the anticommunist paranoia that was rampant in the United States to burn Marshall. He called Marshall's mission to China "the greatest political mistake we made in a hundred years. We will pay for it for generations."

It is sad that Marshall had to suffer such abuse so late in his distinguished career. But the stoicism he had learned as a cadet at Leavenworth and that had been tempered by two world wars and sundry personal tragedies saw him through yet again. Standing fast under fire was "part of the business," and he did it with his customary wisdom and dignity. He wryly referred to his persecutors as the "lunatic fringe," and their jealous and vindictive attacks were soon overshadowed by the bestowal of an honor that finally did true justice to the character of George Marshall: In 1953, he learned that he was to receive the first Nobel Peace Prize ever given to a professional military man.

Five-star general George Marshall died at the age of 78, on October 16, 1959. His funeral, as he had wished, was short and simple. Those who worked with Marshall remembered him as the most self-contained individual they had ever known. Throughout his life, Marshall was a modest man who did his best for his country. He did not seek personal honor or advancement but only to be true to himself and his country. Even at the end of his career he never craved recognition, and he always seemed startled or embarrassed when it was given to him. General Bradley once told a story that is emblematic of this quiet American who gave so much and expected so little in return: Bradley and Marshall had been appointed delegates to the coronation of Queen Elizabeth II in London. As the two men walked down the aisle of Westminster Abbey to their seats at the front, row after row of distinguished international guests rose to their feet. Startled, Marshall turned and looked behind him. "Who are they rising for?" he whispered. "You," replied Bradley.

An honor guard stands watch over the casket of George C. Marshall in the Washington National Cathedral, October 19, 1959. On receiving news of Marshall's death, Winston Churchill stated simply, "He was the last great American."

Further Reading

Acheson, Dean. *Present at the Creation: My Years in the State Department.* New York: Norton, 1987.

Bland, Larry I., and Fred L. Hadsel, eds. *The Papers of George Catlett Marshall,* Vol. 1, *The Soldierly Spirit.* Baltimore: Johns Hopkins University Press, 1981.

———. *The Papers of George Catlett Marshall,* Vol. 2, *We Cannot Delay.* Baltimore: Johns Hopkins University Press, 1986.

Brogan, Hugh. *The Pelican History of the United States.* New York: Penguin, 1987.

Ferrell, Robert H. *George C. Marshall: 1947–1949.* Totowa, NJ: Cooper Square, 1966.

Johnson, Paul. *Modern Times: The World from the Twenties to the Eighties.* New York: Harper & Row, 1985.

Joll, James. *Europe Since 1870: An International History.* New York: Harper & Row, 1973.

Jones, Joseph. *The Fifteen Weeks.* New York: Viking, 1955.

Larrabee, Eric. *Commander in Chief: Franklin Delano Roosevelt, His Lieutenants & Their War.* New York: Harper & Row, 1987.

Leavell, J. Perry, Jr. *Harry S. Truman.* New York: Chelsea House, 1988.

Marshall, George Catlett. *Memoirs of My Services in the World War.* Boston: Houghton Mifflin, 1976.

Mosely, Leonard. *Marshall: Organizer of Victory.* London: Methuen, 1984.

Pogue, Forrest. *Education of a General: 1880–1939.* New York: Viking, 1963.

———. *Ordeal and Hope: 1939–1942.* New York: Viking, 1966.

———. *Organizer of Victory: 1943–1945.* New York: Viking, 1973.

———. *Statesman: 1945–1959.* New York: Viking Penguin, 1987.

Puryear, Edgar F., Jr. *Nineteen Stars: A Study in Military Character and Leadership.* Novato, CA: Presidio Press, 1981.

Sked, Alan, and Chris Cook. *Post-War Britain: A Political History.* New York: Penguin, 1985.

Chronology

Dec. 31, 1880	Born George Catlett Marshall in Uniontown, Pennsylvania
1901	Graduates from Virginia Military Institute
Feb. 3, 1902	Receives commission to the U.S. Army
Feb. 11, 1902	Marries Elizabeth ("Lily") Carter Coles
April 12, 1902	Departs for the Philippines on the *Kilpatrick*
1904	Stationed at Fort Reno Army Base, Oklahoma
1906–10	Receives training at the Infantry and Cavalry School at Fort Leavenworth, Kansas; graduates first in his class
Aug. 14, 1916	Attains rank of captain
1917	United States enters World War I; Marshall serves in France
1918	Central Powers surrender; World War I ends
April 1919	Marshall becomes "Black Jack" Pershing's aide-de-camp (until 1924)
1924–27	Serves in China
Sept. 15, 1927	Lily Marshall dies
Nov. 19, 1927	Marshall becomes assistant commander at Fort Benning, Georgia (until 1932)
Oct. 15, 1930	Marries Katherine Tupper Brown
Aug. 24, 1936	Attains rank of brigadier general
Sept. 1939	Hitler invades Poland; Marshall is sworn in as chief of staff
Dec. 7, 1941	Japan attacks Pearl Harbor
Dec. 8, 1941	United States declares war on Japan, officially entering World War II
Jan. 3, 1944	Marshall is named "Man of the Year" by *Time* magazine
May 1945	War ends in Europe
Aug. 1945	United States drops atomic bomb on Hiroshima, Japan; Japanese government capitulates
Jan. 21, 1947	Marshall is named secretary of state
June 5, 1947	Gives Marshall Plan speech at Harvard
July 1948	European Recovery Program (ERP) goes into effect
Jan. 3, 1949	Marshall resigns as secretary of state
July 1950	U.S. troops enter Korean War
Sept. 14, 1950	Marshall becomes secretary of defense
Dec. 10, 1953	Receives Nobel Peace Prize
Oct. 16, 1959	Dies

Index

Wendy Lubetkin is a senior editor at *World Link*, the magazine of the Geneva-based World Economic Forum. She holds graduate degrees from the London School of Economics and the Columbia School of Journalism and has worked for *Time* and *Money* magazines in New York. She is also the author of *Deng Xiaoping* in this series.

Arthur M. Schlesinger, jr., taught history at Harvard for many years and is currently Albert Schweitzer Professor of the Humanities at City University of New York. He is the author of numerous highly praised works in American history and has twice been awarded the Pulitzer Prize. He served in the White House as special assistant to Presidents Kennedy and Johnson.

PICTURE CREDITS

AP/Wide World Photos: p. 107; The Bettmann Archive: pp. 34, 39, 44, 82, 94; Library of Congress: p. 40; George Marshall Research Library: pp. 16, 17, 18, 19, 20, 21, 22, 24, 27, 28, 32, 36, 41, 48, 53, 59, 65, 68; National Archives: pp. 29, 42, 43, 50, 57; Oklahoma Historical Society: p. 30; Donna Sinisgalli: p. 100; Springer/Bettmann Film Archive: p. 69; UPI/Bettmann Newsphotos: pp. 2, 12, 15, 26, 31, 33, 38, 60, 63, 67, 71, 72, 76–77, 78, 81, 84, 86, 87, 88, 90, 92, 93, 95, 96, 99, 101, 102, 103, 104, 106